Venus: Don't Go There

Venus: Don't Go There

What Science and Religion
Reveal about Life after Death

VENUS: DON'T GO THERE

The permission for use of Bible passages is from the following website: http://www.ncccusa.org/newbtu/permiss.html.

New Revised Standard Version Bible, copyright 1989, Division of Christian Education of the National Council of the Churches of Christ in the United States of America. Used by permission. All rights reserved.

iUniverse books may be ordered through booksellers or by contacting:

iUniverse
1663 Liberty Drive
Bloomington, IN 47403
www.iuniverse.com
1-800-Authors (1-800-288-4677)

ISBN: 978-1-4917-4699-8 (sc)
ISBN: 978-1-4917-4700-1 (e)

Library of Congress Control Number: 2014918526

Print information available on the last page.

iUniverse rev. date: 08/12/2016

Cover: Transit of Venus from NASA
Solar Dynamic Observatory
June 6, 2012
Goddard Space Flight Center

To my daughter,
Veronica Santini,
who created many happy memories during her
childhood upbringing (birthday, April 12)

In memory of
Maria Santini (1936-2012),
my beloved mother, who tirelessly raised her children
and remained dedicated to their well-being

CONTENTS

Chapter 3

Chapter 4

Chapter 5

Chapter 6

ILLUSTRATIONS

Figures

TABLES

PREFACE

There are no ordinary individuals in society. Every person has an immortal aspect to his or her being, a soul that will live on forever after death. Yet, as physical beings residing on the earth, our existence is exceedingly short. Our time in history as functioning humans is a fragile and fleeting commodity. With that in mind, what purpose would an individual on the planet have except to decide one's eternal future and prepare for eternity? Here today and gone tomorrow, the self moves on to an everlasting destiny.

When visiting the cemetery to pay respects to loved ones, I occasionally walk around considering the burial places of unfamiliar people. In my mind, these departed souls are alive and well, with memories and feelings fully intact. A particularly engaging headstone or epitaph will cause me to muse. One question coming to mind concerns the eternal fate of the individual. I ask myself, "Where did this person go, heaven or Hades?"

To speak of heaven as our home is not a figure of speech. Jesus tells us in John 14:2 that he has gone to "prepare a place for you," a forever dwelling that a person can call home. Heaven is where we belong. Death has no power over the believer. The loss of a loved one may bring grief, but the transition from life to death is simply a door, a pathway to a new life free from pain and sorrow. The glory of the destination supplants the process of the passing. The faith-filled person will encounter

God face-to-face after departing this world and experience unsurpassed joy, peace, and splendor. But what can be said of the unfaithful, those who have failed to properly prepare?

The alternate fate is certainly one of gloom and despair. All our work, all our toil, and all our efforts to make the best of life on Earth can end in disaster because of spiritual neglect, unbelief, and hard-heartedness. Hell is a destiny to be avoided at all costs. You simply do not want to go there. Because of inattentiveness to the seriousness of sin, people find the idea of hell irritating and hard to accept. Human transgression is a grave matter before God that goes over our heads. One's sin is boundlessly bad because it is against an infinitely great and holy deity. Consequently, the exacting penalty for being found guilty is a never-ending sentence.

Working years ago in aerospace on a classified space program, I was on travel in Los Angeles for several days to engage in a series of engineering meetings with another defense contractor.[1] During one particular gathering, some dapper young engineers were discussing a design topic. And then it started. Every fifteen to twenty minutes someone would say, "Where the hell is the data?" or "Who the hell is responsible for that?" or "When the hell are they going to finish?" or "What the hell was he thinking?" It quickly became apparent that this brash, cliquish group of professionals was joking about hell. Hell may be many things, but it is definitely not funny.

The last six years of work in aerospace included going to school at night to earn an MA degree from Fuller Theological Seminary. From start to finish and including summer months, my free hours and weekends were filled with reading theology

---

1 Twenty-five years of aerospace engineering work at Lockheed-Martin and Boeing brought opportunity for travel in order to integrate major defense systems. The plethora of funding for large defense contracts is normally spread to suppliers, subcontractors, associates, and teammates around the country. Meeting technical requirements and coordinating schedules for delivery of various components and support services is essential to the success of a program.

books and writing papers. Supplementing my knowledge of the Bible with a formal education was a valuable experience. The effort built a solid foundation for full time doctoral study following retirement. In retrospect, the time and energy spent slowly absorbing rational and systematic views of God aided immensely in understanding how to properly interpret the scriptures.

This book proposes to lay out a reality of perdition that is in complete alignment with the Bible and that people may grasp clearly. Hell is the isolated, future abode of condemned spirits, which is to be feared and avoided. Hell is not imaginary in any sense. In fact, consider hell so real as to likely be on another celestial body, the nearby planet in the solar system called Venus. After final judgment, Venus can become a never-ending place of anguish and abandonment for demonic spiritual beings and for unsaved humanity. For those who do not acknowledge God and who choose to express amusement and indifference toward hell, sequestering to another world, especially this world, will be no laughing matter.

As mortal beings, we have limited perception into the immortal aspects of existence. People are generally unqualified to make judgments concerning eternal matters. We are totally dependent on God to give proper foresight on the subject. Fortunately, the word of God is not silent concerning the afterlife. In the Gospels, Jesus speaks about heaven. He also happens to author the original doctrine of hell. This text will examine His warnings and description of perdition, making the details come alive inside our solar system. I am prayerful that those who are uncertain about their eternal destinies consider the message. Heaven is a beautiful place, and no one, not a single soul, should miss it.

ACKNOWLEDGEMENTS

Research for this book began in earnest during the fall semester of 2011, shortly after dissertation submittal to the faculty of San Francisco Theological Seminary. Much of the learned discipline for writing a major thesis contributes to the ability to rationally formulate and organize the body of this text.

My thankfulness goes out to Sanna Reinholtzen, Carole Della Penna, and Larry Dale, who provided editorial coverage for the book. Their careful review aided immensely in the final release.

Express appreciation to artist Paul Martin, who willingly took on the challenge of creating imagery for the locust invasion of Revelation chapter 9.

Sincere gratitude goes to Joel Hamme for his review of Greek and Hebrew language usage.

Many thanks go to Keith Jones for his coordination and production of graphic art for the text.

Finally, I would like to give thanksgiving to the insight and leading of the Holy Spirit. The researching, organizing, and composing of this volume is in cooperation with the Lord Jesus Christ.

INTRODUCTION

The Rosetta stone of ancient Egypt was the irregularly shaped, black granite rock that bore inscriptions of the Egyptian and Greek languages. The discovery of the engraving in 1799, and the eventual deciphering by the 1820s, led to a permanent bridge of understanding for the multitude of Egyptian hieroglyphic writings. The birds, animal characters, and other symbols of the ancient Near East culture can now be interpreted by archeologists and historians. The stone's imprints faithfully decode Egyptian hieroglyphics found in pyramids and other historical sites.

Though not nearly as comprehensive as equating two languages, this writing discusses 1) scientific innovation and terminology, and 2) various theological and biblical viewpoints. Explaining the interdisciplinary confluence in one instructive text requires a similar bridging. The teaching of two diverse fields of practice is made while comparing and contrasting one another. This necessitates understanding the jargon in each area. With this in mind, a glossary has been added to the latest release. The list of vocabulary words provide clarification, and are taken from the theological, geological, chemical, and space science fields.

Readers require awareness to the idealistic thinking of the "men of science" and the doctrinal persistence of the "men of religion," because misgivings in each field have widened a rift that should otherwise not exist. A major theme of this writing is to accept in real terms that God ordains science and religion to work together. However, the resistance to affinity between these two disciplines is great. As Max Planck once surmised, "A new scientific truth does not triumph by convincing its opponents and making them see the light, but rather because its opponents eventually die, and a new generation grows up that is familiar with it." This is not to imply the field of science is correct in every assertion, but simply to point out that human pride only fades when the final breath has been taken.

The latest release of *Venus: Don't Go There* provides minor revision and update, and well as improved guidance to the original publication of November 2014. One modification is the underscoring of the inner planet as a persuasive model for perdition, rather than being a precise location. The slight redirecting helps guide the reader toward hell being a physically existing place in the universe, and therefore, a place to be avoided without further delay. Though small in scale over the preceding two years, spacecraft exploration and findings have been updated, as dissemination of information moves into the public domain.

It is recommended for the reader to refer to the glossary while going through the list of terms below. As you grasp an understanding of the meaning, you will see theological and scientific views emerging for comparison and contrast.

The author believes in...	Not just...
Revelation (general) Natural Theology	Revelation (divine)

The Bible warns against...	And does not imply...
Eternal punishment	Annihilationism Universalism

The Bible faithfully teaches...	Science arguably teaches...
Creationism (divine)	Evolution (natural)

The author embraces…	And refutes…
Old earth creationism	Young earth creationism

> A proper view of old earth creation recognizes the historicity of Adam and Eve.

This means accepting…	And rejecting…
Creationism (progressive)	Evolution (theistic)

The text clarifies the…	While denying the…
End of the age	End of the world

The space science section uses…	And is less concerned with…
General Relativity Special Relativity	Quantum Mechanics

The writing holds to traditional Christian views, while putting biblical teaching, space science, and geology into conversation with one another. The book maintains the truth of Genesis, while also showing how its verses make room for accepting that our universe is billions of years old. As such, the work ultimately rejects young-Earth theories, as this belief creates a chasm between science and religion. Arguments for the eternal separation of the unrighteous in hell or the lake of fire are made, in keeping with what the scriptures teach.

Additional terms setting the stage for the reader include…

Celestial Heaven
Hades
Hell
Immortal Spiritual Body

Intermediate State
Lake of Fire
Soul

Understanding the origin and future of the universe, as well as doing textual analysis of Genesis and Revelation, will help bridge science and religious over the billions of years since creation. Using physical laws, the book proposes heaven, Hades, and the lake of fire to materially exist within space and time. Biblical exegesis surmises that in the future, heaven is to be located on Earth; and that in the present, Hades is within Earth's inner core. Although Venus is a highly probably location for the unrighteous after final judgment, it remains a conjecture, in light of many other exoplanet destinations within the Milky Way galaxy and universe.

Following the evangelical pattern, the author accepts the divine inspiration, trustworthiness and authority of the Bible in matters of faith and conduct. In creating and preserving the universe, God has endowed our world with contingent order and intelligibility, which is the basis for scientific investigation. Recognizing the dominion the Creator has bestowed upon his creation as keepers of the planet (Gen 1:26), scientific discovery and technological innovation are to be used for the good of civilization and advancement of the entire world.

In conclusion, we move confidently into the body of the text acknowledging and appreciating that we live on an exclusive planet. The establishing hand of the Creator now guides and cares for this world. In rare fashion, the earth is capable of supporting a vast taxonomy of complex living organism. The wonder of our world sharply contrasts the mediocrity principle of accepting nothing unusual or distinctive about our planet's place in the cosmos. God's providence has manifest in biological complexity and intelligent life, which has set apart our globe as a special place in the solar system, the galaxy, and even the universe.

ABBREVIATIONS

The following is a list of acronyms, symbols, and abbreviations in the text.

AVO	Akatsuki Venus Orbiter
CHZ	circumstellar habitable zone
CO_2	carbon dioxide
COS	carbonyl sulfide
CMBR	cosmic microwave background radiation
CPU	central processing unit
ESA	European Space Agency
Gr.	Greek
GPS	global positioning system
Heb.	Hebrew
H_2S	hydrogen sulfide
H_2SO_4	sulfuric acid
IAU	International Astronomical Union
IUS	inertial upper stage
JAXA	Japan Aerospace Exploration Agency
KJV	King James Version
N_2	nitrogen
NASA	National Aeronautics and Space Administration
NKJV	New King James Version
NRSV	New Revised Standard Version
PPM	parts per million
SAR	synthetic aperture radar
SO_2	sulfur dioxide
STP	standard temperature and pressure
STS	space transportation system
USSR	Union of Soviet Socialist Republics
UV	ultraviolet
VeSpR	Venus spectral rocket

BIBLICAL REFERENCES

Unless otherwise noted, the text references the New Revised Standard Version (NRSV) Bible translation. The NRSV sets a standard for the twenty-first century by drawing on newly available sources. These sources include the Dead Sea Scrolls, other newfound manuscripts, archaeological finds from the ancient Near East, and new insights of Greek and Hebrew grammar. The NRSV is available in a standard edition, with or without the Apocrypha. The approved Roman Catholic edition uses the same text as the Protestant publication. A Common Bible version is available, which includes all books belonging to the Protestant, Roman Catholic, and Orthodox canons.

CHAPTER 1

Venus Enters the Church

The heavens are telling
the glory of God;
and the firmament
proclaims his handiwork.

Psalms 19:1

By the will of God, all things were created and have their being.
By His command, the heavenly bodies came into existence; the
vast expanse of interstellar space, galaxies, suns, the planets
in their courses, and this fragile Earth, our island home. From
the original elements, God brought forth the human race,
bestowing upon them memory, reason, and skill. He made us
rulers of creation, with providence, self-sufficiency, and the
ability to reason and to imagine. As intelligent and curious
beings, we look beyond the terrestrial to the celestial, asking
the question, "What is the purpose of this all?"

The setting of the sun is picturesque to singles, to couples
walking hand-in-hand, to the young and old alike. As physically
confined yet incurably inquisitive beings, we stare in wonder
at moonlit skies and dark, starry nights. Across the firmament

extends a seemingly infinite number of celestial bodies of varying brightness, forming identifiable constellations such as the Big and Little Dipper, Hercules, Orion the hunter, Cassiopeia, and Pisces. Asterisms such as the Pleiades generate folklore tales with seven sisters. The night sky stirs our imagination. Stargazers dream of Star Trek voyages into deep outer space, asking theatrically, "Scotty, are you there? Beam me up!"

As demonstrated by the Hubble Space Telescope, one can truly be amazed by the diversity of celestial objects in the universe. From the multiplicity of nebulas to swirls of galaxies, Hubble manages to uncover a kaleidoscope of stunning panoramas in the firmament. From the ground, the telescopes of amateur astronomers pan the night sky searching for a double star or to examine specific features of a planet in the solar system. In the midst of exploration, one can take time to appreciate the goodness and majesty of the Creator for bringing such glorious, immeasurable space.

The irony to the splendor of the night sky is the adverse, foreboding, and inhospitable setting of deep space. Without oxygen and the environmental control system of a space suit, a human cannot survive beyond our earthly surroundings. Our friendly planet provides a safe haven, but beyond the upper atmosphere, adversity looms. Therefore, beyond heaven and Earth, one might find abodes for physical and spiritual beings less than appealing. And if the terrestrial conditions of a planetary body align with the biblical descriptions of perdition, a person might take notice of that condition. From there, one can organize a scientific and faith-based presentation arguing the planet Venus as a model for perdition, the eternal place of spiritual separation for unsaved people.

In the gospel narratives, Jesus establishes the existence of hell as a location set apart for the unrighteous. Yet theologically, the idea of perdition as a permanent, physical place of separation endures skepticism. One reason may be the lack of biblical imagery concerning places such as hell and the lake of fire. Unfavorable speculation about a dreadful destiny away from all that is good can make the concept difficult to grasp, unthinkable or even fictional. In order to restore a sense of reality to this place of exile, we will take a close look at biblical passages and the planetary environment of Venus.

The Nature of Revelation

How does an infinite God provide revelation to finite humanity? How does He disclose information about Himself in order to communicate with His creation? Two recognized approaches are through divine and general revelation. Divine revelation relies on the self-disclosure and communication of God by God to convey knowledge of God to humans. For example, the biblical scriptures are an essential part of the trustworthy record of divine self-disclosure. General revelation, on the other hand, is the self-disclosure and communication of God through means such as observation, experience, innate conscience and reason, as well as the scriptures.

Saint Thomas Aquinas, the great scholastic theologian of the thirteenth century, gave strong support to general revelation in his formulation of natural theology. He maintains there is a valid, objective revelation of God attainable in nature, history, or human personality. The construct can be made apart from the Bible. Truth about God is actually present within the creation and does not necessitate evangelism or the testimony of individuals. Rather, knowledge of God is arrived at through nature by reason, that human capacity to uncover, to comprehend, to interpret, and to evaluate the truth.

Aquinas believes natural theology to be valid, when understanding the limitations of one's awareness. The knowledge gained will be *incomplete, mediate*, and *analogous*.[2] Information will be true, but lack in fullness. For

---

2   R. C. Sproul, *The Consequences of Ideas: An Overview of Philosophy* (Orlando, FL: Ligonier Ministries, 1998).

example, when staring into the vastness of the night sky, one might say, "If there is a God, He is infinite." God is definitely an infinite being, but in what way? Natural theology is *incomplete* in that it cannot tell us God's forgiveness is limitless toward repentant people. Nevertheless, the observation of the physical universe can bring a certain amount of discernment about God.

Natural theology being *mediate* means the idea is being transferred through the surroundings. The revelation of God is not directly from God but comes through a mediator; that is, through creation. The night sky, acting as a medium, conveys knowledge of the divine. Natural theology being *analogous* means comprehension of God can come through correspondence to the natural world. God being unlimited is an attribute that correlates to the unfathomable depths of space. The idea of an immeasurable God does not depart from the intent of the scriptures.

For divine revelation, the Christian life relies primarily on the reading of sacred Scripture. If one carefully considers what the Bible has to say, it can lead and guide a person through life. One can increase in knowledge through revelation from the Word. In 2 Timothy 3:16–17, Paul states, "All scripture is inspired by God and is useful for teaching, for reproof, for correction, and for training in righteousness, so that everyone who belongs to God may be proficient, equipped for every good work." God's principles jump off the page to encourage, to enlighten, and to give daily instruction.

One example of divine revelation unfolds in the body of the New Testament. Jesus describes hell as the "eternal fire" (Matt. 18:8) and where "the fire is never quenched" (Mark 9:48). Another descriptor for perdition is "lake of fire," which is used in Revelation. The book of Revelation is filled with metaphors, so it is not unusual to use lake of fire as a substitute for hell. The torment of those in the lake of fire is "forever and ever" (Rev. 20:10). The lake of fire is where unsaved people go after

Judgment Day. In understanding Hades to be the temporary residence of lost souls, hell and the lake of fire become one as perdition - the permanent place of eternal separation.[3]

Avenues of general revelation can come in those quiet moments of prayer and contemplation. When the mind is settled, the spirit of a person receives prompting and direction through the power of the Holy Spirit. The expression "God whispers" relates the idea that the still, small voice of the Lord God has spoken to the heart and inner conscience (1 Kings 19:12). An idea or series of thoughts can come to mind unexpectedly, and if consistent with the character of God or the intent of Scripture, can be of divine origin. Hearing God's voice in this manner requires a calming of the constantly churning mind.

God can use any number of people to convey His message of truth to us, whether it is through a friend, coworker, parent, pastor, or teacher. Print or broadcast media such as books, songs, e-mail messages, and television programs can contain answers to prayer, or comforting thoughts, or direction. James 3:17 reads, "But the wisdom from above is first pure, then peaceable, gentle, willing to yield, full of mercy and good fruits, without a trace of partiality or hypocrisy." Having a listening ear for godly advice is essential.

The scriptures also address communication that comes through spiritual gifts, such as the Word of Knowledge. The Apostle Paul addresses the receiving of spiritual gifts by the church in 1 Corinthians 12:7–11, in order for the assembly not to remain uninformed.[4] The Spirit is the one who activates these

---

3 The idea of the "lake of fire" being hell derives from the imagery of unquenchable fire. The fire correlates to the constant burning of refuse at the disposal site of Hinnom outside of Jerusalem. Walter A. Elwell, ed., *Baker Encyclopedia of the Bible* (Grand Rapids, MI: Baker Book House, 1988), 1,299.

4 Spiritual gifts are extraordinary abilities that the Spirit gives to believers to build up the church. Michael D. Coogan, ed., *The New Oxford Annotated Bible: New Revised Standard Version* (New York: Oxford University Press, 2001), 285 [New Testament].

gifts in order to provide wisdom, knowledge, faith, healing, miracles, prophecy, tongues, interpretation of tongues, and spiritual discernment to God's people. The bestowing of these manifestations is for the common good. A Word of Knowledge, for example, can be given by a parishioner through divine disclosure, in order to edify or to encourage the ecclesia.

In Joel 2:28 of the Old Testament, the prophet Joel foretold of the coming of the Holy Spirit, stating, "Then afterward, I will pour out my spirit on all flesh; your sons and your daughters shall prophesy, your old men shall dream dreams, and your young men shall see visions." In chapter 2 of the book of Acts, the Apostle Peter's sermon ushers in the church age on the day of Pentecost, while quoting Joel's prophetic message. God has a plan to communicate with individuals in dreams and visions during the church age. The method is a valid pathway for God to speak to His people.

The Bible illustrates the giving of knowledge for insight and practical implementation to individuals through dreams and visions. In the Old Testament, Abimelech receives a warning in a dream to return Abraham's wife (Gen. 20:7). The prophet Daniel receives understanding of Nebuchadnezzar's dream (Dan. 2:1) in a night vision (Dan. 2:19). Joseph, one of the twelve sons of Jacob, dreams prophetically about the stellar life he would eventually live. His dreams come to fruition when he becomes second-in-command of all of Egypt.

In the New Testament, Joseph receives direction in a dream to take Mary as his wife (Matt. 1:20). Dreams guide him to flee to Egypt (Matt. 2:13) and to later return (Matt. 2:19). Ananias assists the Apostle Paul in receiving his sight because of a divinely inspired vision (Acts 9:10–12). Paul receives direction to preach the gospel in Macedonia as the result of a vision (Acts 16:9–10). Dreams and visions, contained in multiple passages of the narrative of Scripture, provide critical pieces of knowledge to aid God's people at the right time and place. The images serve as a source of revelation.

Cultural opinions about the meaning and purpose of dreams have shifted over time. Psychotherapist Sigmund Freud considered dreams to be unconscious wishes or desires, seeking fulfillment. His protégé, Carl Jung, went on to counter many of Freud's theories. Jung considered dreams to be messages to the dreamer containing revelation that helps to resolve problems or fears. Today, the understanding of dreams and visions ranges from cautiously pessimistic to spiritually significant. In spite of differing opinions, it is important to remember that the biblical narratives weigh in favor of paying attention to the underlying messages of dreams and visions.

Theological views of divine and general revelation filter from seminaries to religious institutions to churches, eventually forming specifically held doctrine. At the same time, individuals remain free in how to perceive the divine. The fundamental question becomes: Can revelation of God come through Scripture or the natural world or both? Consider what Paul says in Romans 1:19–20 as being true today: "For what can be known about God is plain to them, because God has shown it to them. Ever since the creation of the world his eternal power and divine nature, invisible though they are, have been understood and seen through the things he has made."

Venus as Hell/Lake of Fire

The book title, *Venus: Don't Go There*, is an honest and straightforward caution about a known, undesirable location. The sun and all orbiting objects came into existence from nebulous material. The formation of the solar system began with the gravitational collapse of a giant molecular cloud. The center formed the sun, while the remainder flattened into a rotating circumstellar disk, which created the planets, moons, asteroids, and other small bodies in our solar system. Although neighboring Venus grew to be nearly the same size as Earth, its evolutionary processes molded a decisively different planet.

As will be discussed later in this text, Soviet spacecraft in the 1970s and 1980s were able to deploy descent modules through the Venusian atmosphere to the ground. Operating on the surface of Venus for only a few short minutes, camera systems took clear, intelligible images of the planet's landscape. The majority of the Venusian surface appears to have been shaped by volcanic activity. The scientific data gathered from the Mariner and Venera programs were the first to detail the planet's uninviting and extremely unpleasant environment. The conditions create a hot, dreary, barren place of exile for the lost.

The book of Revelation, scribed by John the Apostle, gives God's end-time plan for humanity. The text is also called the Apocalypse, which means disclosure or unveiling. The figurative language of the last book of the Bible has mystified readers throughout the history of Christianity. Nevertheless, one should not assign a broad-brush, "warm and fuzzy" feeling to the complex series of events. The writing is not intended to be an indiscernible, utopian text written only to provide general comfort and reassurance to the believer. Activities connect in a sequential progression that is coherent throughout the chapters, leading to a final crescendo before the return of Christ.

Understanding the symbolism of Revelation can bring theological reflection and doctrinal refinement to the current understanding of eschatology. Eschatology, "the study of last things," is concerned with what is believed to be the final events of history. When the events relate to death, resurrection, and eternal destiny, it is considered as individual eschatology. The final three chapters of Revelation are a particularly important part of individual eschatology, as it pertains to the final judgment of humanity and the establishment of a new heaven and new earth.

As part of the final judgment, the reader encounters the term "lake of fire" in Revelation 19:20; 20:10, 13–15; and 21:8. The passages are as follows:

Revelation 19:20: And the beast was captured, and with it the false prophet who had performed in its presence the signs by which he deceived those who had received the mark of the beast and those who worshiped its image. These two were thrown alive into *the lake of fire that burns with sulfur.*

Revelation 20:10: And the devil who had deceived them was thrown into *the lake of fire and sulfur,* where the beast and the false prophet were, and they will be tormented day and night forever and ever.

Revelation 20:13–14: And the sea gave up the dead that were in it, Death and Hades gave up the dead that were in them, and all were judged according to what they had done. Death and Hades were thrown into *the lake of fire.* This is the second death, *the lake of fire;*

Revelation 20:15: and anyone whose name was not found written in the book of life was thrown into *the lake of fire.*

Revelation 21:8: But as for the cowardly, the faithless, the polluted, the murderers, the fornicators, the sorcerers, the idolaters, and all liars, their place will be in *the lake that burns with fire and sulfur,* which is the second death."

In the original Greek language, the word lake (*limneen*) means harbor or waterfront. A body of water can suggest an unchanging or homogeneous surface condition. For example, one can grasp the uniformity and expanse of a large body of water by standing on the calm shore of a large lake. When one looks out onto the glassy surface toward the horizon, the scene is uniform and unvarying. Venus's terrestrial landscape brings a similar consistency over a long distance, only on a dry surface. Volcanism is evident globally on the planet, creating a vast and seemingly unchanging field of view.

The word fire (Gr. *purós*) can be representative of Venus's extremely hot landscape, which records an average temperature of 864°F. The atmosphere has a fast-moving cloud cover, which completely blankets the planet. The clouds retain the suns heat in a greenhouse effect, facilitating isothermal conditions. This means Venus maintains approximately the same temperature around the globe, whether day or night. *Purós*, from which the word pyrotechnic derives, can also refer to lightning, which occurs frequently on Venus as a result of chemical reactions in the atmosphere.

One can grasp another notion of a lake of fire by viewing the cover of this book, which shows the transit of Venus that occurred on June 6, 2012.[5] A planetary transit happens when either Mercury or Venus crosses directly between the sun and the earth. Venus transits are rare astronomical events, with the 2012 event being the last one of the twenty-first century. As Venus courses across the fiery surface of the sun, one can imagine the planet immersed in a lake of fire.

A significant factor relating the lake of fire to Venus is the fact that the planet is teeming with hot sulfur. In the NRSV Bible, Revelation 19:20 and 21:8 tell the reader that the lake of fire "burns with sulfur" and "burns with fire and sulfur." Similarly in the KJV, the passages read "burning with brimstone" and "burneth with fire and brimstone."

Brimstone is an old, nonscientific name for sulfur, an extremely abundant, non-metallic element in the Venusian world, appearing either in elemental form or in chemical combination.

---

5   The dramatic photo was taken from the NASA Solar Dynamic Observatory. The transit occurred while researching and writing this text.

Sulfur is multivalent, denoting the tendency of the element to form other compounds. It bonds easily with other atoms or molecules to create stable and often pernicious substances.

The atmosphere of Venus divides into thermal zones to facilitate the continuous sulfur cycle. On Earth, the water cycle describes the constant movement of water on and above the planet. The same is true for the sulfur cycle of Venus. For example, the atmosphere is primarily carbon dioxide (CO_2) and nitrogen (N_2), but houses trace levels of sulfur dioxide (SO_2) from volcanic outgassing. The copious cloud cover is composed primarily of sulfur dioxide and sulfuric acid (H_2SO_4) droplets. Additionally, the volcanic rocks on the surface contain elemental sulfur.[6]

Close examination of Revelation 20:13–14 is important for a better understanding of the biblical language. The beginning of the passage states "the sea gave up the dead." People who die at sea have no remains. Even in skeletal form, the preservation of physical bodies is not possible at sea. Ocean tides and currents scatter corpses, which settle at varying locations and depths. Fish and crustaceans consume the decaying flesh and bone.

The sea transcends a mere body of water. In first-century Europe, maritime travel was a dangerous affair. Merchant sailor and passenger loss of life was a common occurrence in the vast, uncharted waters. The oceans were an unconquerable and fearful nemesis. The Apostle John's allusion to the sea is to an all-consuming place of turbulence and uncertainty.[7] Ultimately, the giving up of the dead will come from beneath the sea floor.

---

6   Soviet spacecraft descent modules used x-ray florescence spectrometers to assess the overall chemical composition of surface rocks, which contain measureable levels of sulfur. V. L. Barsukov ed., *Venus Geology, Geochemistry and Geophysics: Research Results from the* USSR (Tucson, AZ: The University of Arizona Press, 1992), 166.

7   When the beast rises from the "sea" in Revelation 13:1, the waters are considered to be a place of primeval chaos. The sea represents a place of unruliness and unrest. Coogan, *New Oxford Annotated Bible*, 437, 446 [New Testament].

The scripture then refers to both Death and Hades giving up the dead. The use of "Death" (Gr. *Than'-at-os*) is as a noun in personification. Death has dominion over body and soul. To the lost soul, death means separation from God. The condition of a departed soul in perdition is a tremendous personal loss. Death is to be displaced from Earth and relocated to the lake of fire, which is portrayed as the second death (Rev. 21:8). The threatening force of Death will be sent to another planet. It is a far cry from when the divine presence comes down from heaven to be on Earth, so that "Death will be no more" (Rev. 21:4).

The use of "Hades" (Gr. *Hádees*) can be either as a dark spiritual domain or a physical place of confinement. As will be discussed, the physical location of Hades is near the center of the earth. The souls of the unrighteous remain there until the Day of Judgment. In Revelation 20:14, the NRSV uses the word "Hades," while the KJV uses the word "hell." Fortunately, the New King James Version (NKJV) revises the word from hell to Hades, which is the proper term. One must not confuse Hades and hell. To the first-century person, Hades was the underworld abode of the dead. It continues today as a place of captivity.

As a final point in discussing the passages, Revelation 20:15 and 21:8 pertain to individuals coming up out of Hades to have a life review by God. After the evaluation, making the grade requires having his or her name inscribed in the book of life. At the time of the final judgment, souls resurrected from the underworld will be equipped with an immortal spiritual body. A material resurrection, as understood in the resurrection of Jesus Christ, comes to every person, regardless of whether one has done good or evil (John 5:29).

In the Gospel of Matthew, Jesus begins an important teaching with the Sermon on the Mount (chapters 5–7). The event occurs early in His ministry. The sermon emphasizes moral instruction and contains the basic tenets of Christian discipleship. In these passages, Jesus introduces the term "hell" to the audience as a final punishment for the wicked. The context for this first reference to hell concerns anger toward others, which can manifest in lasting feelings of hate or even retaliation. Failing to ameliorate or correct the mind-set can lead to the spiritual death of the person.

The word hell translates from the Greek word *Gehenna*, but originally sources from the Hebrew as the place called "Hinnom." The valley of Hinnom was a disposal site situated in a deep, narrow gorge southeast of Jerusalem. Originally, it was the area where idolatrous Israelites sacrificed their children to the gods Moloch and Baal. Conducting these immoral and wicked acts was part of worshipping the deities of Semitic culture. Gehenna eventually became the proverbial dumping site for the city's garbage. The location, identified as Tophet in Jeremiah 7 and 19, was a place where child sacrifices were offered and dead bodies burned or buried after death.

In Nehemiah 3:14, we read of the rebuilding of the Dung Gate at the southern end of Jerusalem. People moved dung and collected trash through the gate for burning in the valley of Hinnom. Unlike modern disposal sites that differentiate between garbage and toxic waste, Gehenna accepted every form of refuse. Israelites regarded the valley of Hinnom as a place of devastation and loss, due to the deposit of dead bodies, including animals, criminals and enemies slain in battle. Never-ending burning kept the accumulation of corpses and rubbish in check, although these activities led to offensive sights and foul smells in the valley. Over time, the negative images of the dumpsite became associated with everlasting destruction and fire.

Like the word "hell," the idea of being thrown into a "lake of fire" conjures up destructive images in the minds of individuals. Is this an actual sea of flammable liquid burning incessantly? Are the immortal spiritual bodies of unsaved people literally tossed off a precipice into some inferno? Since a full explanation is not provided, the human mind is free to fabricate atrocious images.

13

Beyond the lack of biblical details, the problem magnifies because hell and the lake of fire are eternal destinations. One purpose for the writing of this book is to address this difficulty and to show that God provides rational and morally principled solutions, even to places such as hell.

Individuals lacking a clear understanding of hell or the lake of fire liken it to a black hole. One hears the use of the term in an arbitrary or capricious way. In a real sense, black holes cannot be applied practically to the scriptures. Black holes are large, dark regions in the space-time continuum. A stellar black hole forms when a massive star ends its life in a supernova explosion. The remaining star matter collapses back in on itself, resulting in a compacted core. The extreme high density results in a gravitational pull wherein nothing can escape. A black hole contains a boundary called an event horizon, marking the "point of no return." Incredibly, photons of light have no rest mass, yet even these elementary particles are drawn into black holes.

Astronomical observation strongly indicates the center of every galaxy may contain a massive or supermassive black hole. In studying the orbits of stars near the center of our galaxy, the Milky Way, scientists have uncovered a massive black hole inside of Sagittarius A, a bright and highly compact radio wave emitter. The strong gravitational pull of the black hole acts as a hub for the rotation of surrounding stars in the galaxy.

Extended viewing times into intergalactic space by orbiting telescopes have uncovered the activities of black holes. In elliptical galaxy RXJ1242-11, x-ray observations revealed a star being ripped apart and sucked in by a supermassive black hole.[8] The text will review empirical evidence for the soul having

---

8   Detection of the event was reported in 2004 by two orbiting space telescopes. One was the NASA-sponsored Chandra X-ray Observatory; the other was the ESA-funded X-ray Multi-Mirror Mission (XMM-Newton). NASA, *Giant Black Hole Rips Apart Unlucky Star in Cosmic Reality Show*, http://www.nasa.gov/home/hqnews/2004/feb/HQ_04061_black_hole.html (accessed August 13, 2013).

physical mass in chapter 4. With this understanding, it is difficult to believe spiritual beings cast into a black hole would be able to survive. The characteristics of these celestial objects cannot reasonably connect to biblical perdition.

Some theologians and Bible teachers attempt to explain that hell and the lake of fire are outside our existing realm of space and time, and as such, are beyond a coherent grasp of the mind. This line of thinking is neither constructive nor biblical, and is certain to draw conversation on the subject to a close rather quickly. Scripture teaches that perdition is tangible. Assigning a location for the ultimate fate of the unsaved does not need to go beyond conception by the human intellect. A planet such as Venus can solidify the idea of what constitutes hell and the lake of fire in our known universe.

Hades exists in the realm of space and time as well. The text deduces the physical location of Hades to be the same as the Old Testament location of Sheol. It is within the earth. Historical support for Hades as an underworld place of exile for unsaved souls is in the systematic theology of Charles Hodge, principal of Princeton Theological Seminary from 1851 to 1878. Hodge believed in all points that the Greek idea of Hades corresponded with the Hebrew notion of Sheol, the underworld destination of departed souls.[9] He uses the parable of the rich man and Lazarus in Luke 16 as a key reference for his belief. Sheol/Hades is a distinct underground setting designed for separation from God's immediate presence.

In Matthew 16:18, Jesus uses the word "Hades" in commending Peter, "And I tell you, you are Peter, and on this rock I will build my church, and the gates of Hades will not prevail against it." In this application, Hades takes on the sense of a formidable evil empire. The Lord views the spiritual domain of Hades to have agency geared toward rebellion, hostility, and wickedness.

---

9   Charles Hodge, "Systematic Theology – Volume III", http://www.ccel.org/ ccel/hodge /theology3 (accessed June 7, 2012).

Satan and his demonic army dwell within the spiritual domain of Hades, which spans the entire earth. It is distinct from physical Hades, which is basically a holding tank in the depths of the underworld, where unrighteous souls and confined demons are kept. The spiritual domain of Hades engages in cognitive, spiritual battle with Almighty God, the holy angels, and the earth's inhabitants.

Acknowledging Hades to have "gates" brings concern when applying a first-century understanding to the passage. Gates were robust and thoughtfully planned fortifications of ancient Near East cities. Therefore, the spiritual domain of Hades is understood as a fortified and resilient operation, with an established hierarchy. The spiritual terrain is amorphous in shape, powerful in sway, and vast in size, covering the far reaches of the planet. Satan leads the dark forces of the spiritual domain of Hades into continual conflict with the light of the kingdom of God. The spiritual domain of Hades is organized to accuse, to criticize, and to condemn God's people in the established church age.

After the final judgment, perdition awaits evil spirits and lost people. Venus can become the final destination of Satan and his demonic army, the beast, the false prophet, and all unsaved humanity. The demonic beings of the global spiritual empire of Hades are cast out. The fallen angels remaining in physical Hades are thrown into the lake of fire as well. The discarding of the geographic location of Hades in the center of the earth is like emptying a cardboard box. You can dispose of the material inside and still keep the container. The contents within the physical borders of Hades empty out, but the enclosure remains in the core of the earth.

The church has traditionally taught about Satan, sin, and the catastrophic fate of the unsaved, but present-day churchgoers hear less and less on this foremost topic. When was the last time you heard a preacher give a "fire and brimstone" sermon on the fate of the lost? With a great sigh of relief, many will say,

"Not in a long time." In the closing decades of the twentieth century, the topic of perdition seems to have disappeared from the pulpit. When finally hearing a sermon on the subject, silence grips the audience. Hell is an unpleasant and fearful place. Many people have close and loving associations with family, friends, and neighbors who have rejected the gospel message.

Dialogue on heaven and hell has experienced neglect because clergy and laity alike tend to focus more on the here and now. Finding fulfillment in the present day matters a great deal to the modern churchgoer. Living the Christian life with an eye on eternity does not draw great interest in an American culture geared toward financial success and the accumulation of material goods. Topics with a futuristic twist, such as the rewards of heaven or the consequences of hell, are not popular with the congregation. Over time, the biblical heaven becomes ethereal, and hell is relegated to an artifact of times past. Yet, many passages of Scripture teach of gaining the eternal perspective by laying up treasures in heaven and avoiding the consequence of hell.

One problem in understanding the hereafter is the lack of biblical imagery. Scripture does not explore and enlighten the reader on the milieu of heaven and hell. As such, these places become mysterious, abstract, ever so distant from reality, and seemingly lacking in concreteness. Venus brings tangibility to the subject of perdition through interdisciplinary study, which combines two or more academic disciplines into one research project, creating something new through the crossing of boundaries.

The following sections give a basic, introductory overview of applicable information for the scientific aspect of this study and include some brief personal history. The first segment, astronomy, discusses the configuration and types of planets in our solar system. The second section is an abbreviated review of the history of space exploration. In studying the planetary

17

journeying of various nations, it turns out that Venus is one of the most visited bodies in the solar system. The third part regarding artificial satellites addresses spacecraft design and operation. The term "artificial" distinguishes orbiting man-made objects from natural satellites such as the moon. Voyaging spacecraft have gathered much data and achieved great understanding of the Venusian environment.

Astronomy

The Remick Observatory is on the grounds of Lockport High School in Lockport, New York. As a member of the Astronomy Club, I would go to the observatory in order to peer through the optical telescope, and then peruse the small adjoining planetarium. Memorizing facts about the planets and finding the location of constellations was part of the fun. Friends from high school would share enthusiasm for space and astronomy. Teachers and students not only enjoyed the splendor of a beautiful starry night, but also desired a greater understanding of the heavens.

Back in the late 1960s and early 1970s, the nine recognized planets were Mercury, Venus, Earth, Mars, Jupiter, Saturn, Uranus, Neptune, and Pluto. At the time, knowledge about the planets in the solar system, the spiral arm structure of the Milky Way, and the composition of matter and energy in the universe was limited. The ensuing decades brought continual enhancement in telescope technology. The launch of the Hubble Space Telescope and other artificial satellites built for space exploration would help dramatically to improve information about our galaxy and the universe.

One example of increased knowledge in our solar system is in the number of moons revolving around the planets. At the time of my high school graduation in 1973, Jupiter had 12 moons identified in its orbit, Saturn had 10, Uranus had 5, Neptune had 2, and Pluto had none. Today, the number of natural satellites on

Jupiter and Saturn exceeds 60 confirmed orbits, with Uranus, Neptune and Pluto numbering 27, 14 and 5 respectively. Particularly small natural satellites known as moonlets, with a diameter of a half mile or less, have been identified in the ring system of Saturn and in minor-planet moons.

The 1992 discovery of the Kuiper Belt opened up new categories and definitions for planetary objects. The Kuiper Belt, which extends outward beyond Neptune, is a region of smaller-sized, icy rock bodies and dwarf planets in heliocentric orbit. Resulting from the discovery was the 2006 downgrade of Pluto to a minor or dwarf planet by the International Astronomical Union (IAU). The demotion was primarily due to a portion of Pluto's orbit being closer to the sun than neighboring Neptune. The IAU definition of a planet requires it to "have cleared the neighborhood around its orbit."[10] The elliptical track of Pluto crosses Neptune's course, disqualifying it from status as a conventional planet.[11]

Under the newly established classification of planets by the IAU, there are currently eight planets and five dwarf planets in our solar system. Besides Pluto, the minor planets of Ceres, Haumea, Makemake, and Eris classify as dwarfs. Technically, there are thousands of minor planets in the solar system, but only five receive recognition at this time. Ceres is located in the asteroid belt between Mars and Jupiter. Reference to this object is sometimes as a large asteroid, rather than a dwarf planet. Haumea, Makemake, and Eris are trans-Neptunian bodies that lie in the Kuiper Belt with Pluto.

---

10 International Astronomical Union, "Resolution B5: Definition of a Planet in the Solar System," (*XXVIth IAU 26ᵗʰ General Assembly*, (Prague, Czech Republic): IAU, August 24, 2006), 1.

11 For sentimental reasons, some state governments and amateur astronomers rejected the Pluto downgrade. Most members of the scientific community agree with the change. International Astronomical Union.org, "IAU 2006 General Assembly: Result of the IAU Resolution Votes," http://www.iau.org/public_press/news/detail/iau0603/ (accessed February 28, 2012).

Our solar system contains two different types of planetary worlds: terrestrial planets and gas giants. Terrestrial planets have crusts that are composed primarily of silicate rocks and metals. The word "terrestrial" derives from the Latin *terra*, which means "land" or "earth." The planets Mercury, Venus, Earth, and Mars are terrestrial planets. Terrestrial landscapes have features such as craters, volcanoes, canyons, mountains, and plains. The planets have similar internal structural composition consisting of a metallic core, a surrounding silicate mantle, and compact, rock-strewn surfaces. The lunar plains present a volcanic landscape that reflects the appearance of a terrestrial planet.

Gas giants such as Jupiter and Saturn are composed primarily of thick atmospheres of hydrogen and helium. Uranus and Neptune are technically referred to as ice giants, a subcategory of gas giants. Ice giants are composed of hydrogen and helium but contain more "ices" such as water, ammonia, and methane. The vast majority of "gas" and "ice" in the interior of these planets is actually in the form of a hot fluid. The gases compact and become increasingly dense descending toward the center. Due to the lack of a hard surface, space exploration of gas giants consists mainly of orbiting and flyby vehicles.

The final frontier of planetary science is in the exploration, discovery, and study of exoplanets or extrasolar planets; that is, planets outside our solar system. Scientists have supposed the existence of extrasolar planets for centuries, but were unable to confirm their existence until the mid-1990s. With the launch of the Kepler space observatory in 2009, a goal of which was to detect Earth-size planets in the habitable zone, the number of documented exoplanets in the Milky Way has grown exponentially. The data from the mission has spawned several studies by astronomers, including a January 2013 report by the California Institute of Technology (Caltech) that conservatively estimates there are at least 100 billion exoplanets in the Milky Way.[12]

Space Exploration

Formal space exploration began during the political Cold War era between the United States and the Soviet Union. The launch of Sputnik 1 in October 1957 placed the first artificial satellite into Earth's orbit. The USSR-built spacecraft was shaped like a large silver sphere with four long, whip-like antennas protruding from its head. A month later, a female dog named "Laika" boarded Sputnik 2 and became the first animal to orbit the planet. The United States responded in February and March 1958 by launching Explorer 1 and Vanguard 1. These mission successes began a technology race between the two countries, ushering in the space age.

The first person to venture into outer space was cosmonaut Yuri Gagarin of the Soviet Union. On the historic date of April 12, 1961, his Vostok 1 spacecraft performed a single orbit of the earth and completed a successful landing in 108 minutes, marking the first time a human had entered outer space. Following closely behind this event was American astronaut John Glenn, who orbited the earth three times on February 20, 1962, in Friendship 7, a Mercury spacecraft launched from Cape Canaveral, Florida. Propelled by an Atlas LV-3B vehicle, the mission lasted slightly less than five hours.

In the years following Yuri Gagarin's historic flight, the Soviet cosmonaut became an international celebrity, parading throughout the Soviet Union, visiting countries around the world, and receiving numerous honors and awards. The date of

---

12 A minimum of one planet orbiting around each star in the Milky Way could place the number of exoplanets as high as 400 billion in our galaxy. California Institute of Technology (Caltech), "Planets Abound," http://www. caltech.edu /content/ planets-abound (accessed April 22, 2013).

April 12 became a designated holiday known as Cosmonautics Day, which Russians still celebrate today.

Interestingly, the NASA launch of the first Space Shuttle mission (STS-1) was twenty years to the date of Vostok 1, on April 12, 1981. With these two achievements in mind, space fans celebrated Yuri's Night exactly twenty years later, on April 12, 2001. It was a "world space party" honoring human spaceflight. In 2011, the United Nations General Assembly adopted resolution A/RES/65/271 declaring April 12 as the International Day of Human Space Flight. The day is now celebrated annually around the world to commemorate the beginning of the space era for humankind.

Over the years, the development of reliable and more efficient boosters resulted in thousands of successfully launched space vehicles. The registry of space missions includes NASA's Apollo program of manned voyages to the moon. The initiative to "land a man on the moon and returning him safely to Earth" achieved its goal by the end of the 1960s.[13] To date the moon is the only place in the solar system that humans have visited, with six spaceflights bringing twelve men to the lunar surface by the end of 1972.

Through the decades, unmanned space vehicles launched by various nations have explored outer space, gathering information about the earth's surroundings. The primary purpose of sending spacecraft to nearby planets is to increase human knowledge of the physical characteristics and composition of these bodies. Space vehicles explore adjacent worlds searching for a better understanding of the evolutionary processes of the earth, the solar system and the universe. Two favorite targets of multiple spaceflights have been Venus and

---

13 The pragmatic commitment to achieve the objective of putting a man on the moon was made to the nation by President John F. Kennedy during a joint session of Congress. John F. Kennedy Presidential Library and Museum, "Excerpt from an Address Before a Joint Session of Congress, 25 May 1961," http://www.jfklibrary.org/Asset-Viewer/xzw1gaeeTES6khED14P1lw.aspx (accessed March 1, 2012).

Mars. Historically, the Soviet Union has put strong effort toward exploring Venus, while the United States has directed more investigation toward Mars.

Today, hundreds of satellites circle the globe, their geocentric orbits varying in altitude, inclination, and eccentricity. The primary purpose and mission of these artificial satellites is to protect, improve, and modernize civilization, assisting people in almost every part of the world. The genesis for the design and implementation of spacecraft originate from government agencies and commercial enterprises. Services provided by satellites include their use in Global Positioning System (GPS) for location and navigation; surveillance and reconnaissance for national defense; telecommunication for television, radio, and cell phones; and climate monitoring for predicting weather changes, which can warn of impending dangers such as hurricanes and tornadoes.

Satellite Design and Operation

Knowing about the operation of spacecraft and their payloads is helpful when examining the chronicles of space voyages to Venus and other planets. In the available literature on solar system exploration, a majority of discussion is about space vehicles undertaking interplanetary voyages to achieve specific mission objectives. Some of the literature is for the general reader, while other information is directed at the technically minded person.

In order to assess all the data, it is advantageous to have a general understanding of spacecraft mission planning, operational requirements, subsystem design configuration, instrumentation, experiments, and intended communication between space and ground. The terminology is familiar to aerospace engineers and is part of comprehending the overall history of space travel to other planets.

The term aerospace forms from two words. The first part,

aero, is from *aero*nautics, which is the science of flight within the atmosphere. The second, *space*, is the realm including both the earth's atmospheric envelope and beyond. Aerospace engineers work within two physical domains to design and build objects for flight, including airplanes, rockets, missiles, and spacecraft.

Satellite systems, built for commercial and military application, orbit the earth collecting and relaying information to users around the globe. It takes years, sometimes more than a decade, to evolve from the concept phase to being fully operational. The stages necessary to produce and to eventually operate a space vehicle include (1) the concept and design phase, (2) the part procurement and manufacturing phase, (3) the development and test phase, (4) the launch event, and (5) the final operational phase, where communication and tasking of the satellite occurs.

The building of spacecraft mandates meeting the design specifications. Approved test procedures contain requirements needing to be verified from specification requirements. Successful qualification requires testing of procedures that replicate operational use in the space environment. The requirements test electrical and mechanical functionality, as well as the software interface. The test verification process helps to ensure the spacecraft will survive the dynamic launch environment and operate successfully in the harsh space environment for the intended duration of the mission.

A colloquial term used for one of the high-level spacecraft assembly testing sequences is "shake and bake." As part of verification testing, shake and bake simulates the launch vibration and thermal environment the space vehicle will experience during the mission. Acoustic testing uses massive speakers to shake the structure with sound vibration. The baking portion places the vehicle in a special vacuum chamber to simulate space. The mechanical structure, electrical components, and wiring of the spacecraft experience hot and cold temperature cycling, in order to ensure thermal controls are functioning properly.

The test engineering effort requires an understanding of the overall requirements and constraints, environmental conditions, space vehicle subsystems, and mission objectives. Primary subsystems of the spacecraft bus operate in full support of the mission payload. The payload can consist of any number of components. It can include down-link and cross-link antennas for relaying data, contain scientific experiments, or accommodate various pieces of equipment for earth surveillance.

Spacecraft must withstand titanic forces during vertical liftoff. The assembly sits on top of a launch vehicle that is powered by rocket motors using solid or liquid propellant. In order to protect the space vehicle from the dynamic pressure and aerodynamic heating of atmospheric ascent, it is encased by a payload fairing, or the external nose cone. The fairing is normally made of three vertical sections that are mechanically stitched together. Once the booster reaches the upper atmosphere, the fairing pyrotechnically unzips along the seams with the pieces being jettisoned by the aerodynamic forces.

The power of the liftoff must work against Earth's gravitational attraction. In order to overcome the effects of gravity, the thrust, or g-force level must exceed the pull of the planet. As an example, astronauts on board the Space Shuttle would normally experience a 3g force during ascent. Beyond the atmosphere, orbiting satellites must survive the extreme conditions of space, including a high vacuum environment and radiant heating and cooling. Thermal effects in a vacuum will cause "touch temperatures" on the sun side of vehicles to approach 250°F and the dark side to be as cool as -200°F.

Satellites operate independently to accomplish program objectives, with intermittent use of mission control commands to deploy or move electro-mechanical appendages, point antennas, download payload data, relay control information to the ground, turn different electrical subsystems on and off, or reestablish various operating modes in the computer control system.

In addition to satisfying mission requirements, satellite programming includes housekeeping tasks and recovery functions. For example, if an anomaly causes the spacecraft to perform a sudden, unplanned maneuver, the attitude control sensors will signal the onboard computer. The central processing unit (CPU) will then begin an emergency systematic shutdown of the satellite that reduces electrical power to a subsistence level.

The secure shutdown from the CPU will include a spacecraft maneuver to point the solar array panels toward the sun, while directing the downlink antenna toward the earth in order to await further commands. Pointing the solar arrays at the sun provides continuous power to the batteries for great lengths of time. Known as safe-hold, this survival mode of operation ensures the protection of the satellite from catastrophic loss until vehicle control personnel at the ground station can analyze telemetry data and resolve the anomalous condition. The necessity for trustworthiness of these autonomous, interwoven and nuanced control features is reason for stringent spacecraft testing.

CHAPTER 2

Biblical Views of Perdition

*All scripture is inspired by God,
and is useful for teaching,
for reproof, for correction, and for
training in righteousness*

2 Timothy 3:16

The Bible has many wonderful things to say about inheriting the blessedness of eternal life. Jesus began His earthly ministry by proclaiming the good news about the kingdom of God being at hand. His primary mission was to tell people about a heavenly Father who loves them and has prepared a place for them. The paradise of heaven is the pinnacle of supreme happiness and peace, where God and the holy angels dwell. It is a glorious place of bliss, the ultimate fulfillment of the deepest human longings.

As a secondary feature of the teaching, Jesus speaks about the fate of those who choose to ignore the call to salvation. His sermons are full of care, tenderheartedness, and compassion toward the multitude. Yet, He alerts the religious hypocrites and the wrongdoers of impending judgment. Instead of going

27

to heaven, people can choose hell by failing to give ear to the message. Perdition serves as a place of separation from God and results in suffering, due to being absent from everything good. All good sources in God and being cut off from that goodness can only result in serious deficiencies.

While researching this book, I found myself saddened and even demoralized about the subject of hell. It is not a pleasant topic to contemplate. As a result, I would pick up a diametrically opposed text about heaven to cheer myself up again. Contemplating heaven and hell affected my state of mind, but they are not simply conditions infused into one's psyche. Heaven and hell are real places; that is, physical locations residing within the universal dimensions of space and time. Scriptures gives strong evidence that immortal beings can dwell in our physical space.[14]

The Bible provides a consistent testimony to the gravity of human sin and the inherent consequences of death resulting from sin. In comprehending the topic of sin and death, one must remember the Bible teaches in a manner that always leads to the truth. Personal and communal sin is a pervasive problem in the scriptures. It is a known, recognized condition of fallen humanity. One learns to understand the incurable human propensity to sin and the antithesis of God's holy being. The message is basic; people have to come to terms with the dilemma of wrongdoing in order to find the right relationship with God. This is where the simple message of the gospel comes into effect.

For the unprepared individual, a huge risk presents itself. Since depictions of hell are of an inescapable place of misery and loss, one ought to give serious consideration to one's

---

14 The transfiguration of Jesus, along with the sudden appearance of Moses and Elijah, demonstrates the ability of the immortal spiritual body to reside within universal space. Peter goes on to suggest the building of three tabernacles to preserve the experience (Mark 9:2–5). Coogan, *New Oxford Annotated Bible*, 75–76 [New Testament].

eternal state and plan accordingly. Human life is fragile and our time on the earth is short. Though the present moment is fleeting, the average person spends little time thinking about his or her ultimate destiny. The unavoidable reality is that our bodies are hopelessly stuck in the natural world, unable to break away from impending death and decay. The earthbound state dictates a birth into a life that will eventually conclude in passing away and appearing before a higher power.

According to the latest statistics, 56.7 million people die every year.[15] The data translates into 108 deaths per minute, or almost 2 every second. The fate of the departed soul is either ascension to a paradise filled with eternal joy and happiness or descent to a sequestered place of sadness and regret. The news media gives attention to catastrophes that take scores of lives at once. Going unnoticed is the moment-by-moment procession of death in the world.

God's revelation of Himself is progressive in the Bible. Leafing back through the Old Testament can serve as a reminder of how judgment comes to sinful people. The scriptures generally speak of divine wrath in response to human transgression. One primary historical event is the flooding of a region of the earth after only ten generations of human existence.[16]

The deluge was a sweeping sentence of the creation brought on by drastic circumstances. The number of people committing wicked and immoral acts had continued unabated, growing to enormous proportion. Because of the condition, the

---

15 The crude death rate is 7.99 deaths / 1000 of population (2012 estimate). CIA World Factbook, "Library Publications: People and Society," https://www.cia.gov/library/publications/the-world-factbook/geos/xx.html (accessed March 5, 2012).

16 One interesting biblical debate is the geographical extent of the flood, which did not need to be global in order to accomplish its purpose. Human beings occupied only a fraction of the planet when Noah constructed the ark. Geological evidence points to a massive deluge occurring over the expanded region of Mesopotamia. Reasons to Believe, "The Waters of the Flood," http://www.reasons.org/articles/the-waters-of-the-flood (accessed February 5, 2014).

Lord God was single-minded toward driving the population to extinction. Only Noah, his family, and representative pairs of animals were to be spared.

One can view the divine retribution of sudden physical death as a judgment upon corrupt human beings. Surprising to some readers is the severity of the punishment by a holy deity; however, it reveals the attitude of the Lord God toward deliberate and continuous disobedience. The offenders gave neither thought to the Creator, nor consideration to sin causing the spiritual separation. They were eating and drinking, marrying and being given in marriage, right up until the flood came and destroyed them all (Luke 17:27). The scene clues readers into God's approach toward the unrepentant and foreshadows final eternal judgment.[17]

In the New Testament era, God's patience toward sin and global wickedness is a function of divine mercy and grace, purchased at the cross of Christ. God maintains compassion, favor, and blessing to mortal creatures in the midst of defiance. One of the intentions of this goodness and longsuffering is for people to understand the depth of His love. God's desire is to keep everyone from eternal condemnation and His prevention plan includes constant doses of kindness and benevolence throughout life.

God allows humans ultimately to control their own destinies. In his book, *The Great Divorce*, C. S. Lewis states, "There are only two kinds of people in the end: those who say to God, 'Thy will be done,' and those to whom God says in the end, 'Thy will be done.'"[18] Lewis believes every lost person has chosen his or her destiny, and that without self-choice, there could be no hell.[19]

---

17 Robert A. Peterson, *Hell on Trial: The Case for Eternal Punishment* (Phillipsburg, NJ: Presbyterian and Reformed Publishing, 1995), 25.

18 C.S. Lewis, *The Great Divorce* (New York: MacMillan, 1946), 69.

19 Lewis maintains people are individually responsible for choices made in life. One's eternal destiny comes about through personal preference. He considers the doors of hell to be locked on the inside. Ibid., 69.

One important teaching in the chapter is that the current location of Hades is below the surface of the earth. The implication of Hades being in the interior of the planet carries forward from the Old Testament understanding of Sheol as an underworld settlement. In the Septuagint, the Greek translation of the Hebrew Bible, "Hades" normally substitutes for the word "Sheol." The final analysis will show that the Sheol spoken about in the Old Testament corresponds directly to the Hades of the New Testament.

Sheol in the Old Testament

The Old Testament does not impart a great deal of insight into the hell of the New Testament, but it does imply afterlife in a place beneath the earth. In the NRSV, the Hebrew word *Sh'owl or Sh'olaah* translates Sheol, "the place of departed souls" or "the state of the dead." At death, Hebrew writers consider all departed souls going to the netherworld of Sheol, a temporary place of confinement and separation from the living. The KJV translates Sheol as "grave," "pit," or "hell." The translation of grave or pit is suitable, but the KJV use of the word "hell" for *Sh'owl* is confusing at best and an incorrect rendition at worst. The meaning of hell as the final place of separation and loss is not introduced until the New Testament.

Sheol is a place where both the righteous (Gen. 44:29) and the unrighteous (Ps. 9:17) go after death. Job considered Sheol a place of conscious existence, as he wishes concealment there until the wrath of the Lord passes (Job 14:13). As a final resting place for self-indulgent and disobedient Israelites, Isaiah reckons Sheol to have a vast appetite and large opening (Isa. 5:14). The destiny of rebellious and idolatrous individuals is frequently associated with Sheol, conveying the notion of confinement for the sinful.

The Old Testament regards descending into Sheol, going down to the grave, or the act of burial in a similar manner.

Sheol is an underground region, a place of darkness within and below the earth. It is in the farthest recess from light. In the rebellion of Korah and his men against Moses, the earth opened its mouth and swallowed the dissenters alive, as they fell into Sheol (Num. 16:30). In describing the fate of Pharaoh and his army at the Red Sea, the Lord God said, "On the day it went down to Sheol, I closed the deep over it and covered it" (Ezek. 31:15). The prayer of Hannah in 1 Samuel 2:6 states, "The Lord kills and brings to life; he brings down to Sheol and raises up." Scripture after scripture consistently portrays Sheol as being under the earth.

The depiction of going down into Sheol ranges from peaceful burial, to drowning, to an aggressive swallowing through a large split in the ground, which is presumably caused by an earthquake. All the openings on the earth's surface are in the downward direction, placing Sheol on a nadir course. Nadir is in the direction pointing straight under a particular location; the spot on the celestial sphere directly below an observer, following the line of gravitational pull toward the center of the planet. Extending the directional path of nadir inferred by burial, drowning, or falling will lead to the core of the earth.

In some passages, Sheol is depicted as a welcome resting place for the faithful servants of Yahweh. In other passages, going to Sheol has a disciplinary flavor, where confinement is an act of early judgment. Sheol is the fully encompassing and invisible world of all departed souls. The apocryphal book of Enoch introduces a division of souls in Sheol when mentioning the idea of discrete "apartments" for the righteous and the unrighteous (Enoch 22:1–14).[20] In expanding the Judaic understanding of the underworld, Jesus alludes to a separation in physical Hades between the good and the evil person in the parable of Lazarus and the rich man.

---

20 The Ethiopian Orthodox Church regards the book of Enoch as canonical. Warren F. Draper trans., *The Book of Enoch* (Andover, MA: U.S. Act of Congress, 1882), 47.

Foretelling of the Prophets

In the entirety of the Old Testament, only two prophets foretell of never-ending problems for the unrighteous person. The verse below closes the final chapter of Isaiah, a prophet who ranks as one of Israel's most significant. In Isaiah 66:22–24, we read,

> For as the new heavens and the new earth, which I will make, shall remain before me, says the Lord; so shall your descendants and your name remain. From new moon to new moon, and from Sabbath to Sabbath, all flesh shall come to worship before me, says the Lord. And they shall go out and look at the dead bodies of the people who have rebelled against me; for their worm shall not die, their fire shall not be quenched, and they shall be an abhorrence to all flesh.

In this passage, the prophet Isaiah looks to the end-times, when all the people of God will come to worship Him on the holy mountain of Zion. The pericope begins on a positive note in verse 22 with its reference to the "new heavens and the new earth." A similar phrase appears in Revelation 21:1 concerning God's home, the holy city of Jerusalem. In the New Testament context, the word "new" translates as *kainos* from the Greek, suggesting the giving of freshness, renewal, or new character to the earth.

The scene then shifts in verse 24 to contrast the fate of the unrighteous. Their dead bodies are understood to be alive and having to cope with an unceasing hardship and a fire that is impossible to put out. The hardship, or worm, is an unspecified type of weakness or suffering. The association of fire or heat with punishment is emblematic of perdition in the Bible.

A second scripture in Daniel implies a final destiny of unending scorn for a rejected group. Daniel was a person of deep piety, whose book contains many end-time prophetic passages. Daniel 12:1–2 reads,

> At that time Michael, the great prince, the pro-
> tector of your people, shall arise. There shall be
> a time of anguish, such as has never occurred
> since nations first came into existence. But at that
> time your people shall be delivered, everyone
> who is found written in the book. Many of those
> who sleep in the dust of the earth shall awake,
> some to everlasting life, and some to shame and
> everlasting contempt.

Similar to the Isaiah passage, Daniel looks to the distant future of Israel and all nations. The "time of anguish" spoken about is a period of unrivaled tribulation in human history, where Michael the archangel will stand guard over God's people. The guarantee of deliverance is having one's name "written in the book," a phrase found in Revelation 20:15, referring to the book of life. Daniel's portrayal of a dual resurrection for the righteous and unrighteous is the only Old Testament reference to such an event. Both groups will rise from the dust, one to eternal life and the other to shame and never-ending contempt.

The awakening of "those who sleep in the dust of the earth" brings to mind the misnomer of "soul sleep"—that period of dreamless slumber between a person's death and the resurrection of the soul. The concept relies primarily on the use of "sleep" as a reference to death in Scripture. The problem with accepting this view is the lack of consistency. Important biblical passages clearly address a person having awareness between death and resurrection.[21] These references work against the idea of accepting sleep as a literal state. Rather, it is best to consider the use of "sleep" as a gentle or reverent way of describing the cessation of life.

The Teachings of Jesus

Compiled into four Gospels are the teachings of Jesus, which provide a written report of His life, death and resurrection. The purpose of the accounts is to announce the arrival of the kingdom of God on earth and to make known the forgiveness of sins. The high point of the narrative is death by crucifixion, where Jesus makes atonement for all past, present, and future sin. The resurrection of Christ foreshadows the new and everlasting life of all who believe in him. After rising from the dead, Jesus appears to more than five hundred people at one time (1 Cor. 15:6). The theme of resurrection in the Gospels points toward rebirth, or renewing of mind and spirit.

John the Baptist was the prophet who paved the way for the arrival of Jesus. His ministry consisted primarily of preaching to address repentance of sin and then performing water baptism. He confronted the Jewish religious leaders of the time, candidly exposing their hypocrisy and self-righteous attitudes. John gave a prophetic warning to the unrepentant in Mathew 3:12 by declaring, "A winnowing fork is in his hand, and he will [thoroughly] clear his threshing floor and will gather his wheat into the granary; but the chaff he will burn with unquenchable fire."

John's discourse frequently contains warnings of judgment

---

21 Three events in scripture counter the notion of soul sleep. First, Saul has a direct encounter with the deceased prophet Samuel in 1 Sam. 28:14–5. Second, Abraham, Lazarus, and the rich man are conversing in the afterlife of a parable of Jesus (Luke 16:19–31). Third, during the transfiguration of Jesus, Moses and Elijah physically appear and engage in dialogue with the Lord (Mark 9:2–5). Coogan, *New Oxford Annotated Bible*, 442 [Old Testament] and 74, 129 [New Testament].

to the religiously pretentious and unrepentant of his day. In this passage, John envisions a futuristic time when Jesus Christ will come to judge the world. It will be an occasion to sift and sort the righteous from the unrighteous. His figurative language is appropriate for the agrarian-based Palestinian culture. Wheat was one of the earliest and most valuable cultivated grains of the Eastern Mediterranean. The chaff surrounding the cereal was of a light, worthless character and was normally disposed of through incineration.

The teaching of Jesus bears much of the burden for the understanding of hell as an eternal place of loss, suffering, and separation. In Matthew 7:13, the Lord states, "Enter through the narrow gate; for the gate is wide and the road is easy that leads to destruction, and there are many who take it." In Matthew 10:28, Jesus tells the disciples, "Do not fear those who kill the body but cannot kill the soul; rather fear him who can destroy both soul and body in hell (*Gehenna*)." His reference to the disposal site in the valley of Hinnom as destruction by fire is fitting for first century Jerusalem.

Many of the warnings of Jesus tend to heighten one's awareness of perdition, as well as instill a healthy sense of concern. God knows the human condition is one of indifference that manifests in spiritual neglect. Without overt admonition, many in a self-seeking and materialistic world would overlook the grace, goodness, and continual love of God. This is why Jesus alerts people to separation and destruction in hell with a plethora of verses throughout the Gospels.

In Mark 9:43–48, Jesus speaks about taking heed not to commit sin and ruin your own soul. The pericope mentions the reprehensible deed of cutting off a hand or foot, or tearing out an eye, if it causes one to sin. A maimed body with one hand or foot is better than an eternity of separation from God. The suggestion to tear out an eye is an atrocious undertaking. Though not meant literally, one can deduce the graveness of hell as the alternate choice to these grizzly acts. The teaching enlightens the audience that sin is toxic, even deadly. Transgression is a serious matter before God, not to be taken lightly.[22]

In speaking to an unrepentant community, Jesus states in Matthew 11:23, "And you, Capernaum, will you be exalted to heaven? No, you will be brought down to Hades. For if the deeds of power done in you had been done in Sodom, it would have remained until this day." Capernaum was a primary dwelling place of Jesus and the disciples, and the site of many miracles during His public ministry. A city having been blessed by His presence and teaching would ultimately face a communal judgment because of unbelief. The indictment carries a heavy price for all the inhabitants. The temporary place of Capernaum in Sheol would occupy a lower tier than Sodom, a city full of moral corruption.

When you depart from this world, you will continue to exist, and where you exist for an eternity depends on the choices made in the here and now. If anyone discounts this notion, then consider Jesus's parable of the rich man and Lazarus in Luke 16:19–31. The story brings reality to life after death, as the narrative portrays dead men in conversation with one another. The audience for this parable is intended as the Pharisees, but the disciples and other followers are likely to be listening. The complete scripture bears repeating for its weightiness and value to the understanding of Hades.

> There was a rich man who was dressed in pur-
> ple and fine linen and who feasted sumptuously
> every day. And at his gate lay a poor man named
> Lazarus, covered with sores, who longed to
> satisfy his hunger with what fell from the rich

---

22 The series of warnings using body parts points to maintaining internal discipline. Temptation should be kept in check and no provision made to sustain immoral behavior. Coogan, *New Oxford Annotated Bible*, 75 [New Testament].

man's table; even the dogs would come and lick his sores. The poor man died and was carried away by the angels to be with Abraham. The rich man also died and was buried. In Hades, where he was being tormented, he looked up and saw Abraham far away with Lazarus by his side. He called out, "'Father Abraham, have mercy on me, and send Lazarus to dip the tip of his finger in water and cool my tongue; for I am in agony in these flames." But Abraham said, "Child, re-member that during your lifetime you received your good things, and Lazarus in like manner evil things; but now he is comforted here, and you are in agony. Besides all this, between you and us a great chasm has been fixed, so that those who might want to pass from here to you cannot do so, and no one can cross from there to us." He said, "Then, father, I beg you to send him to my father's house—for I have five brothers—that he may warn them, so that they will not also come into this place of torment." Abraham replied, "They have Moses and the prophets; they should listen to them." He said, "No, father Abraham; but if someone goes to them from the dead, they will repent." He said to him, "If they do not listen to Moses and the prophets, neither will they be convinced even if someone rises from the dead."

Parables were a common form of teaching in Judaism. Parables communicated by Jesus were instructive, often conveying a profound truth with penetrating ethical implication. I will use the parable to draw attention to eight pertinent points. The exercise is not intended to analyze or extract every aspect of the teaching.

1. The use of the word "Hades" creates parallelism to Sheol, located in the lower regions of the earth. As noted earlier, Hades is the Greek word equivalent of Sheol.

2. Jesus, a man of impeccable integrity and reliability, is teaching that there is life after death. He introduces a partition to Sheol/Hades, a concept unfamiliar to His Jewish contemporaries.

3. In the underworld of physical Hades, the division of abodes is between the righteous and the unrighteous. Lazarus is in Abraham's bosom, a term normally identified with being in heaven or in paradise (Luke 23:43). The rich man is on the torment side of Hades.

4. The rich man's reversal in fortune is due to his lack of compassion for the destitute. His was a heart never made tender by repentance. He feasted lavishly while ignoring the needs of the poor, who wasted away outside the entrance to his home.

5. There is a sense of irreversibility to the damnation of the rich man and the blessedness of Lazarus. It is too late for the rich man to show shame or contrition for his stingy and heartless attitude.

6. The flames cause the rich man suffering, but he receives no relief. Without shielding or protection in Hades, the soul has exposure to high temperature in the center of the earth.

7. The desire for water is so severe on the torment side of Hades that a mere drop from a dangling finger can bring a level of satisfaction.

8. The five living brothers have to rely on the testimony of Moses and the prophets or the "law and the prophets." In other words, the evidence of Scripture and the witness of faithful believers are sufficient proofs.

In the parable, physical death followed by conversation in the next world introduces the audience to the reality of an afterlife. Using the term "Hades" instead of "Sheol" places these worlds in one integrated setting, while pointing to a location beneath the earth. Jesus defines a separation that clearly exists in Hades, where the righteous soul resides apart from the unrighteous. The division is a paradigm shift. The righteous are found in comfort and the unrighteous are found in a place of distress. The teaching emphasizes eternal consequences associated with choices made during one's life.

It is important to understand the present-day configuration of Hades. The righteous residing adjacent to the unrighteous was only a temporary condition. Those of faith no longer dwell in the heart of the earth. Paul affirms believers are absent from the Lord in the mortal body, but after departing this life, they enter the presence of the Lord (2 Cor. 5:6–8). Paul penned these words in his letter to the Corinthians after the resurrection of Jesus. Following the atonement, direct admission to paradise became possible. When believers die today, they have the privilege of promptly entering God's presence.

A spiritual event of cosmic proportion emptied Abraham's bosom. Millions of souls departed from there to enter the heavenly paradise. The relocation to heaven is believed to have taken place in the time between the death and resurrection of Jesus. The undertaking facilitates the removal of the righteous from their underground confinement. The scripture referring to the occasion is Ephesians 4:8–10, which states,

> "When he ascended on high he made captivity it-self a captive; he gave gifts to his people." (When it says, "He ascended," what does it mean but that he had also descended into the lower parts of the earth? He who descended is the same one who ascended far above all the heavens, so that he might fill all things.) [23]

---

23 The Lord enters the heart of the earth in order to access Abraham's bosom. Coogan, *New Oxford Annotated Bible*, 324 [New Testament].

In the New Testament, writers often quote or allude to Old Testament passages. In this case, the scripture can be cross-referenced to Psalm 68:18.[24] The most comprehensive hermeneutical approach is to reflect on the overall theme of Psalm 68, rather than just verse 18. Psalm 68 considers a victorious military leader and the right he has to give the people captured as gifts. In this case, Christ has liberated sinful people by redeeming them.

As the victor, Jesus has the privilege to give those captive in Hades (Abraham's bosom) as gifts to the church body.[25] In order to rescue these individuals, Jesus descends into the earth to gain access to them. The virtuous souls depart from the underworld, being raised by Christ in glory to be with him in heaven. Condemned souls remain behind. The underworld of Hades becomes a place of complete darkness and separation from God.

The primary purpose of Jesus's ministry was to bring the news of the kingdom of God arriving on Earth. Beginning with His forerunner, John the Baptist, and continuing in his preaching, there is an underlying consequence of ignoring the message. His depiction of a wide road to destruction (Matt. 7:13) implies that a great number of people are unwilling to listen, which by default leads to negative consequences. His warnings are open, clear pronouncements of impending suffering and loss. The decision to pay attention to the teaching is in the hands of every individual.

---

24 Psalm 68:18 reads, "You ascended the high mount, leading captives in your train and receiving gifts from people, even from those who rebel against the Lord God's abiding there." Ibid., 832 [Old Testament].

25 John F. Walvoord and Roy B. Zuck, *The Bible Knowledge Commentary* (Colorado Springs, CO: David C. Cook, 2002).

Warning of Paul in the Epistles

The book of Romans takes center stage as the most formal and systematic of Paul's epistles. He places emphasis on our right standing with God being a free gift, received by faith alone. After a salutation and prayer of thanksgiving, the apostle presents a record of human vices. Paul finds people to be completely culpable for the list of transgressions. He argues individuals have a sense of right and wrong and live without excuse because of an innate knowledge of God. The instinctive sense of a higher power makes people guilty.

Later in the text, Paul speaks about the peace, honor, and grace given to those who live by faith. He also addresses a day of wrath, coming to those with impenitent hearts. The apostle writes of the consequences of hell, without explicitly addressing hell itself. This is consistent throughout his letters. Paul portrays perdition as a state of chastisement and exclusion from the presence of the Lord. His warning remains consistent with the gospel's teaching. Every individual who ignores the salvific plan is to receive recompense for his or her deeds. No one will "skate by" the judgment of God.

In writing to the troubled church at Corinth, Paul sees the struggles of a nascent Christian movement. His letter addresses the problems of an assembly exposed to influential and widespread secular thinking. Wrongful speech and behavior from the surrounding community had invaded the body of believers. The city of Corinth was prospering as a commercial success, but the value system of the residents had gone awry.

The ancient seaport was a city-state on the Isthmus of Corinth, a narrow stretch of land that joins the Peloponnesus to the mainland of Greece. Travelers came from around the known world, as Corinth was centrally located between Italy and Turkey. The sojourners were negatively impacting the metropolis in various ways. The debauchery in Corinth was acknowledged to the point where the word *korinthiazomai* (meaning, "to act like a Corinthian") was coined as a synonym for sexual immorality.[26] A young church plant in a corrupt city needed encouragement and reminding of their position in Christ.

Paul addresses the mind set of accepted worldly wisdom in 1 Corinthians 1:18 when stating, "For the message about the cross is foolishness to those who are *perishing*, but to us who are being saved it is the power of God." The apostle contrasts two groups: one on the pathway to destruction and one having attained salvation. Foolish in the eyes of a disoriented world is the idea of a Savior having to undergo crucifixion for the sake of human sin. The lack of acceptance finds root in a system of unbelief that is undergirded by human pride.

In the passage, the word "perishing" comes from the Greek word *apollumi* and means "on the way to destruction." The same term, "perish," finds use in the oft-quoted John 3:16, "For God so loved the world that he gave his only Son, so that everyone who believes in him may not *perish* but may have eternal life." Perishing sharply contrasts eternal life. The word goes beyond the immediate, short-term physical condition of death. It is more than expiring, cashing in your chips, or kicking the bucket. The usage brings a sense of continual devastation in the next world.

In his letter to the Thessalonians, Paul speaks of a day of reckoning for humankind. In 2 Thessalonians 1:9, he states, "These will suffer the punishment of eternal destruction, separated from the presence of the Lord and from the glory of his might." The word destruction (Gr. *olethros*) does not mean obliteration or extinction. As both a conscious and eternal outcome, the devastation entails the prolonged loss of

---

26 Aristophanes of ancient Athens, a comic playwright with the power of ridicule, receives the credit for coining the word *korinthiazomai*. J. Hampton Keathley, "The Pauline Epistles," http://bible.org/seriespage/pauline-epistles (accessed September 28, 2012).

everything worthwhile. An earthly parallel would be the ruin of life and property following an overwhelming and widespread tsunami. The end-time drama will unveil the hidden secrets of everyone; human intent and waywardness will be found out.

In the letter to the Philippians, the apostle speaks of Christ's exaltation in 2:9–11, saying, "Therefore God also highly exalted him and gave him the name that is above every name, so that at the name of Jesus every knee should bend, in heaven and on earth and under the earth, and every tongue should confess that Jesus Christ is Lord, to the glory of God the Father." Inhabitants from three distinct physical locations possess knees and tongues. The act will be done in veneration for some, but for others, out of compulsion.

A final warning in the epistles relates to the distraction of riches. Paul's teaching raises issue with those attached to wealth, for "the love of money is the root of all kinds of evil" (1 Tim. 6:10a). A chronic desire for the accumulation of assets can be a deterrent to finding salvation. Warnings against being stingy, ignoring the needy and adoring money abound in the Bible. Scripture urges people to be generous, to be thankful for what they have, and to direct attention to spiritual matters. In Matthew 6:24, Jesus cautions about not being able to serve both God and money, because undue focus on obtaining wealth distorts judgment. An excessive desire for money and possessions creates a mindset toward the temporal, leaving little or no room for eternal considerations.

The Apocalypse and Final Judgment

Prior to discussing the great white throne judgment of Revelation, it is prudent to mention two other judgments in the New Testament. The first is the weighing of accomplishments and giving of rewards at the judgment seat of Christ. The judgment seat (Gr. *bema*) is the raised seat or platform of a Roman governor or judge. Pilate tried Jesus at the bema in

Jerusalem. The Lord's bema will be a judgment of the righteous, which determines eternal gifting in proportion to one's good works. The scene is in the celestial heaven, prior to the Second Coming of Christ to the earth.

The basis for the judgment seat of Christ is found in 2 Corinthians 5:10, where Paul states, "For all of us must appear before the judgment seat of Christ, so that each may receive recompense for what has been done in the body, whether good or evil." The apostle is reminding the faithful that they are not only on their way to eternal glory but also on their way to being evaluated. Labor akin to wood, hay, and straw is to be burned in the fire while undertakings of gold, silver, and precious stone survive to receive an invaluable reward (1 Cor. 3:12–13). How one invests time in the temporal realm becomes the testing ground for making or marring a destiny, winning or losing a crown.

Another judgment is of the nations in Matthew 25:31–46. The timing of the judgment occurs soon after the Second Coming, where Christ gloriously appears on the earth to usher in His rule for a millennium. The thousand-year reign of Christ is spoken of in Revelation 20:1–7. The judgment of the nations occurs at the end of the tribulation period and prior to the start of the millennial period. The Tribulation is an apocalyptic dispensation that brings seven years of continuous plagues and suffering upon the earth. The return of Christ brings a close to the widespread destruction and devastation.

The nations (Gr. *ta ethnē*) in Matthew 25:32 can be translated "the Gentiles." These are all people, other than Jews, who have lived through the tribulation period. In the Old Testament, the term Gentile applies to non-Israelites, to those not from the stock of Abraham, who were outside God's original covenant. In the New Testament, the Gentiles were to become full citizens and members of God's household. The occasion for review appears to be based specifically on how people treated "the least of these," or those in greatest need. The division of the two groups is between sheep and goats.

The sheep perform good deeds by helping the neediest of persons, all of whom are Christ's brethren. They are given a place of honor and blessing on the right-hand side of the king. These people were faithful in feeding and clothing the poor, welcoming the stranger, nurturing the sick, and visiting the confined. In being blessed of the Father for helping the impoverished, the sheep ultimately receive an inheritance in the eternal kingdom. When I read about these individuals, Mother Theresa comes to mind. She is the quintessential example of a person who sacrifices her entire life to help the poor and the destitute.

Deemed guilty are the goats, who neglect those in poverty. These individuals are given a place of dishonor on the left-hand side of the king. Like the rich man in the parable of Lazarus, these people were negligent in helping the less fortunate, who appear to represent or directly substitute for Jesus. The goats fail to look beyond themselves in order to address the needs of others. Given a place of dishonor on the left-hand side of the king, these people go on to suffer eternal separation from God.

The final eschatological judgment is the great white throne judgment. The judgment occurs at the end of the millennial age, following the casting of Satan into the lake of fire. In chapter 20 of the book of Revelation, John makes mention of a great white throne in verses 11–12, where he states,

> Then I saw a great white throne and the one who sat on it; the earth and the heaven fled from his presence, and no place was found for them. And I saw the dead, great and small, standing before the throne, and books were opened. Also another book was opened, the book of life. And the dead were judged according to their works, as recorded in the books.

Souls held in the underworld receive judgment at the great white throne. From the earlier discussion of Revelation

20:13–15, one understands the people judged to come up from the sphere of Hades. The underground abode of the dead empties entirely of souls and people are brought up out of the ground to a great white throne, located on the earth's surface. These include individuals from every level of society, independent of authority, rank, financial status, or intellectual achievement. The whiteness of the throne is a reflection of the purity and holiness of the One who sits on the throne. Additionally, the color reflects the rendering of justice in an impartial and equitable manner.

The opening of various books, which record the thoughts, words, and deeds of every person, provides evidence for the charges of misconduct and law breaking. Individuals who have heard the gospel and rejected the message must stand alone in attempting to justify various actions. The findings of any evil or wrongdoing will result in condemnation. After the proceedings, the basis for conviction and sentencing is in one's name not being written in the book of life.

Individuals found guilty in the great white throne judgment are to be thrown into the lake of fire. The offenders will have to face an eternal penalty for transgressions. Without an intercessor, lost humans will join Satan, his demonic army, the beast, and the false prophet in the lake of fire. At the great white throne judgment, people under assessment get a glimpse of a beautifully renewed Earth. Once banished from God's presence, individuals will face a terrible change of venue, as they venture to a hot, cloud-covered world of volcanoes and lava fields – a planet such as Venus.

It is important to note that resurrection from Hades to the earth's surface for judgment requires the soul, the afterlife essence of an individual, to be clothed in an immortal spiritual body. The soul is only a transitional state. The second or final eternal state, I call the "immortal spiritual body."[27] When

---

27 Further detail discussion of the soul, the experimental evidence of soul substance, and the immortal spiritual body will be made in chapter 4.

souls from Hades arrive for final judgment, God resurrects the individual through the use of an immortal spiritual body. Whether God deems one righteous or unrighteous does not change the fact that resurrection awaits every individual. The issue is whether the person will spend eternity with or without God.

Annihilationism and Universalism

The idea of permanent loss and eternal separation for the transgressor has biblical foundation, but for many, it raises unsettling concern. Why would a good, benevolent, and loving God allow individuals to experience this eternal fate? How can wrongdoing or spiritual neglect for a temporal time translate into living in a place of exile for an eternity? Are there not theological understandings or interpretations of the Bible that provide a better explanation for the fate of unsaved people following physical death?

In order to develop theological notions, believers in the biblical text utilize not only the scriptures, but tradition, reason, and experience. These four pillars allow guidance for the understanding of God and facilitate the critical pursuit of "faith seeking understanding." In examining Scripture, it is most imperative to do exegesis, which utilizes a three-pronged approach to analyzing the text. The process includes using historical-critical study, implementing proper literary interpretation, and applying reader self-awareness of personal bias or attitudes.[28]

To be avoided is eisegesis, which is the practice of reading one's individual opinion into Scripture, rather than letting the

---

28 Historical-critical method concerns the author's world-view and how the text came to be. It includes the study of history, archeology, anthropology, and topography. Literary interpretation examines the world within the text functioning as language and story. It encompasses genre, grammar, sentence structure, vocabulary, and expression. Reader self-awareness looks at the culture, world-view, presuppositions, values, language, and self-understanding of the investigator.

text rule the perspective on a particular matter. The output of imposing one's own ideas into Scripture has given rise to the concepts of annihilationism and universalism in the field of personal eschatology. These stand-in theologies have always existed in Christendom in one form or another. Unfortunately, the viewpoints have gained prominence in the church over the past several decades.

Annihilationism is the belief that those who die apart from saving faith in Christ will ultimately face a complete end. The immortal spiritual bodies of lost people will disintegrate or be completely extinguished. The total destruction of a spiritual being occurs upon arrival in the lake of fire. This version of annihilationism conceives of a universal resurrection of all persons before final termination. Another form of annihilationism, known as conditional immortality, asserts that the soul contains only the potential for immortality. Guilty souls pass out of existence at the point of death before going to Hades.

The doctrine of annihilationism has existed as a minority view throughout church history but experienced resurgence in the 1980s among some theologians. Annihilationism understands the traditional view of hell or the lake of fire as morally repulsive and condemns a conscious separation and punishment for the lost. Clark Pinnock sums up the view best when stating:

> Obviously, I am rejecting the traditional view of hell in part out of a sense of moral and theological revulsion to it. The idea that a conscious creature should have to undergo physical and mental torture through unending time is profoundly disturbing, and the thought that this is inflicted upon them by divine decree offends my conviction about God's love. This is probably the primary reason why people question the tradition so vehemently in the first place. They are not first of

all impressed by its lack of a good scriptural basis but are appalled by its awful moral implications.[29]

Pinnock claims that the case for eternal punishment does not have strong biblical support. To address the claim, we examine the final verse of the previously mentioned judgment of the Gentile nations in Matthew 25:31–46.

In 25:46, a division occurs between the righteous and the unrighteous. The sheep go on to "eternal life," while the goats head into "eternal punishment." In the passage, the same word for eternal, the Greek word *aionios*, modifies both life and punishment. The meaning of *aionios* speaks to a state of perpetuity, or an everlasting type of condition. Grammatical consistency dictates that *aionios* apply to the eternal condition of both the sheep, who inherit the kingdom, and the goats departing into the eternal fire.

A second example is in the epistle of Paul to the Romans, where he provides warning against an everlasting sentence. He portrays perdition as a just and unending state of punishment, and exclusion from the presence of the Lord. Romans 2:6–11 states:

> For he will repay according to each one's deeds: to those who by patiently doing good seek for glory and honor and immortality, he will give eternal life; while for those who are self-seeking and who obey not the truth but wickedness, there will be wrath and fury. There will be anguish and distress for everyone who does evil, the Jew first and also the Greek, but glory and honor and

---

29 Pinnock's statement classically represents the annihilationism stance. He presents his analysis in the final section of the book titled *The Conditional View*. William Crockett ed., *Four Views on Hell* (Grand Rapids, MI: Zondervan, 1992), 164–65.

peace for everyone who does good, the Jew first
and also the Greek. For God shows no partiality.

Again, one can infer in the scripture a parallel existence in
eternity for both the righteous and the unrighteous. The faithful
doer will find glory and honor when stepping into the next
world. For the self-seeking, who shun the truth of the gospel,
God's wrath and fury will lead to anguish and distress. The
unbeliever will not face annihilation, at least according to the
Apostle Paul.

Pinnock infers a loss of assurance in God's love. His moral
concern for humans undergoing unending torment influences
his thinking. It is completely natural for a person of faith to have
apprehension concerning the fate of the unsaved. One goal of
this book is to help alleviate the worst and most nightmarish
thoughts associated with perdition. As noted earlier, the lake of
fire conjures up all sorts of terrifying scenes of eternal suffering
and agony. Although it is not a good place, I believe modeling
Venus as hell and the lake of fire helps to mitigate a number of
the most unreasonable and frightening prospects.

The vignette in chapter 6 will address the afterlife
condition on Venus. The story brings understanding to biblical
phraseology such as "the worm never dies and the fire is
never quenched" (Mark 9:48), or where "there will be weeping
and gnashing of teeth" (Matt. 8:12). Venus is an unpleasant
location, a planet that is obnoxious and disagreeable in every
regard. Unsaved people will suffer distress inhabiting the
lifeless volcanic domain. Additionally, any place designed for
banishment from the presence of God will not only have poor
living conditions, but will continue to maintain a sinful and
corrupt state of affairs.

The second alternate view of the hereafter is universalism,
the belief that every person will receive restoration to a right
relationship with God and obtain entry into the kingdom of
heaven. The common thread among different types of

universalism thinkers is the final salvation of all humanity. The basis for this belief lies in emphasizing the love and compassion of God. These attributes were clearly on display in the life and ministry of Jesus of Nazareth. His care and concern for every human being cannot be understated. Consequently, universalism proposes God's final victory over evil comes through the reconciliation of all humanity, rather than through exile.

As with annihilationism, the motivation for the unanimous reconciliation of persons originates in the uprising against endless punishment. Universalism finds support at the grass roots level, as well as with pastors and theologians, who come to embrace the doctrine as a pious hope. Having a strong impersonal love for all people, I understand the yearning for universal salvation. Who can find fault with desiring every person to be heaven-bound? We all want deceased family members and friends to be in a better place than life on Earth afforded. The people of the world share the vision of a blissful heaven for departed ones. Yet, universalism is not a clear or evident teaching in the Bible.

Universalism has a long history of prominent supporters. Entering the twenty-first century, it sustains a minor but growing position in Christianity. One current sponsor of a universal type of reconciliation is Pastor Rob Bell, who has authored the popular book, *Love Wins: A Book about Heaven, Hell, and the Fate of Every Person Who Ever Lived*. Bell believes unsaved people will have the continuous opportunity to say yes to God over an indefinite period. He writes:

> Telling a story in which billions of people spend forever somewhere in the universe trapped in a *black hole of endless torment* and misery with no way out is not a very good story. Telling a story about a God who inflicts unrelenting punishment on people because they did not do or say or

believe the correct things in a brief window of time called life is not a very good story.[30]

The use of the expression "black hole of endless torment" conveys that Bell has an unintelligible sense of perdition. He draws a parallel between biblical descriptions of eternal suffering and astronomical ideas concerning black holes, in order to surmise an inaccurate and absurd place for lost people. As noted earlier, the portrayal of a black hole paints a meaningless picture of an immense, highly compacted, and unlivable place. When one considers a place such as the planet Venus, rather than a black hole, as the final destiny of unsaved people, the picture begins to make more sense.

In his book, Bell acknowledges the existence of hell but not as a final resting place. In his understanding, there is a "period of pruning" or "time of trimming" where impenitent individuals experience a correction. His belief lies in postmortem evangelism, which supposes conversion and the grace of God not to cease at death. It is an afterlife where confinement is restorative, even for the worst offenders of society.

Bell maintains an emphasis on the eternal love and compassion of God for every individual. He finds reassurance with the lack of biblical clarity and details concerning the consignment of perdition. The exact type of existence to expect in the afterlife is not known biblically. Consequently, he reacts against the "suffocation of church dogma" and of certitude in personal eschatology.

The universalism of Bell is a doctrine wrought by an imbalance in the character assessment of God, and by the incomprehensibility of hell. On the one hand, the divine nature

---

30 Bell envisions God's love to be greater than any destructive choice made by people. Unlike C.S. Lewis, who understands the free will of individuals to drive eternal destiny, Bell envisions the pre-eminence of God's unconditional love to steer the course. Rob Bell, *Love Wins: A Book about Heaven, Hell, and the Fate of Every Person Who Ever Lived* (New York: HarperCollins, 2011), 110–11.

does have absolute love toward human beings. On the other hand, God has absolute justice toward choices and actions.

The unwillingness to apply intellectual reason to perdition fuels a growing problem being addressed by this book. In the final analysis, the biblical teaching of eternal separation from God needs to be accepted, as the concept is consistently present in the text. If what the Bible teaches is inaccurate or false, then one is free to accept universalism. But no single pastor or theological scholar has enough evidence to the contrary to deny the guidance of Scripture.

CHAPTER 3

Bridging Science and Religion over Time

Lead me in your truth, and teach me,
for you are the God of my salvation;
for you I wait all day long.

Psalms 25:5

The sciences and biblical faith exist to work cooperatively. A rational relationship between the two begins with the creation of the universe, continues today, and will remain far into the future. Each field of study seeks to understand and know ultimate truth. The pursuit of this common goal allows each branch the opportunity to assist the other in grasping the history and future possibilities of the human experience. As a practical, systematic, and intellectually based enterprise, the sciences build and organize knowledge logically through observation and experiment.

The chapter provides past, present, and future evidence of cooperative alliance seen between the physical sciences and biblical theology. It touches upon the life sciences as well. Science assists in the divine directive for humans to be involved in the sustaining and advancement of the created order. As such, science is under the authority of God. Science and religion have been ordained to work together for the common good and to point toward a comprehensive understanding of the future. In doing so, Earth and Venus are understood to remain intact in the solar system after the Lord's return.

Faith and Science as Synergistic

Science begins as a mandate from God to the creature. Genesis 1:28 directs human beings to dress, till, keep, replenish, and subdue the earth. The historical increase in the body of knowledge finds evidence through the progressive tool-making technologies of the Stone Age, the Bronze Age, and the Iron Age. The ability of humans to effectively carry out daily tasks comes through the establishment, development, and implementation of the natural sciences. Science makes use of the theoretical and empirical realms for understanding the makeup and meaning of the physical world, as well as the entire universe.

Since the scientific endeavor is part of the original plan and purpose of the creation story in Genesis, it requires a level of appreciation by members of the clergy and people of faith. The scientific institution is not antireligious, but rather, focuses on the methodical gathering and assessment of observable data in the material world. One should not expect scientific reporting to acknowledge the creative acts of a higher being. Theoretical or experimental scientific reporting will shy away from the metaphysical or the supernatural, while attempting to maintain an objective treatment of subject matter.

One may encounter apparent findings and supposed truths in the natural sciences that run counter to biblical teaching. During these times, it is best to draw appropriate lines of distinction between fact and supposition. One must assess the real evidence coming into play. It is not wise for Christians to agree with every speculation science offers or acquiesce to naturalist philosophy. Yet, we are called to honor and appreciate science as an important discipline, existing for the health and well-being of the creation.

Religion addresses beliefs and practices relating to a supreme being. Understanding the nature and worship of a deity, as well as the involvement of the divine in human life, are part of the spiritual experience. Religion and spirituality have an important function in this world, because creatures of intellect seek direction and purpose for existence. For example, Christian spirituality seeks to discover the gifting of God through traits, talents, and abilities. As one journeys in self-discovery and life experience, the individual grows in awareness of God and in his or her personal relationship to God.

Sacred texts such as the Bible not only address the essentials of salvation but examine thoughts, lifestyles, behaviors, and decision-making processes. An individual can discover the essence of his or her self and relate in a healthier way with others through connectedness to a larger truth. The higher reality of God's loving presence in a person's life can motivate concern for humanity, resulting in the betterment of civilization. The ethical behavior of individuals and the overall moral direction of society, as well as conviction toward meaning and purpose in life, should be of interest to all people.

Saint Thomas Aquinas understood nature and grace to provide valid disclosure about God. Grace is the favor of God, the action of God's merciful disposition toward His creatures. Contained in grace is revelation and knowledge about God that comes through the study of Scripture. Reality concerning God can derive from nature as well. Most intriguing, however, is the insistence Thomas has on there being "mixed articles"— certain truths that can be learned from examining both nature and grace. Thomas creates one of the most influential arguments in church history by way of mixed articles, his five rational proofs for the existence of God.[31]

Thomas held conviction for ultimate truth through nature and grace. The same can be said for science and religion. The disciplines examine the same world through two different lenses, yet can cooperate in uncovering higher truth. A majority of the public, however, sees science and religion as opposing forces. If science becomes more prominent and assertive, then religious faith and spirituality must be less true and have diminishing value. Not so. Science and religion are both valid avenues through which to attain greater knowledge. If conflict exists between the two fields, it exists because of a lack of comprehensive understanding by one or both disciplines.

For example, in spite of a deficiency of solid facts and evidence, scientists insist on proclaiming a primordial soup of amino acids to be the source of complex life on Earth. Without God and through time and chance, life originates and continues to produce new species of higher complexity through mutation and natural selection. Exactly how "natural evolution" fits together over time remains unsolved, as many puzzle pieces are missing. Yet, in fields such as biology, paleontology and geology, affirmations continue as if all the facts are known. The National Science Foundation, a taxpayer-funded institute, relentlessly backs claims of humans evolving from earlier species of animals. For people of faith to question this assertion without more evidence seems reasonable.

And despite obvious and clearly irrefutable data about the observable world, some biblical scholars insist on maintaining uninformed interpretation of Scripture. Rather than accept the

---

31 Thomas gives credence to the existence of God by putting forth the idea that motion must initiate from a separate and distinct source, apart from itself. Movement does not originate on its own, but generates externally, which he attests to be God. In applying the thought to cosmic creation, one can see God as the initiator of an expanding universe. Saint Thomas Aquinas, *Summa Theologica* (New York: Benziger Brothers, 1947), First Part, Question.2, Article. 3.

clear facts about the age of the universe and our home planet, religious tradition disregards the evidence and maintains a condensed time period for the creation story. Better theology through spiritual enlightenment needs to come to the church. Religion can work cooperatively, in partnership, or even operate synergistically with science, in order to satisfy the vital curiosities of the human intellect.

Science cannot address essential questions relating to human existence. For example, science cannot explain why human beings are the only species that has highly developed reason or why the world is ordered and open to rational investigation. On the other hand, religious texts do not provide answers in the natural realm, such as how the human circulatory system operates or what works to provide cures to certain diseases. The Bible lacks specific answers in many fields, though it is of divinely inspired origin and authority.

Chronologically, the tension between science and religion began a few centuries ago. Many historians like to point to the Italian astronomer Galileo Galilee's discovery and proclamation to the church that the earth was not at the center of the universe. Adopting Copernican heliocentrism, Galileo understood the earth and planets to be rotating around the sun, with the sun being near the center of the known universe.

The astronomical observation occurred in the early 1600s, a time when the first working telescopes came into use. Galileo's findings conflicted with the accepted wisdom of the age, including the thinking of the Roman Catholic Church. Having adopted an earlier version of geocentricism known as the Ptolemaic system, the church was dogmatic in its opinion of the earth's centricity. It took centuries for the church to admit the error, with the resulting dissention creating an estrangement between science and religion.

Astronomy is the scientific study of celestial objects and observable phenomena originating beyond Earth's atmosphere. Astronomers gaze across the universe to examine the motion and nature of objects such as comets, planets, stars, and galaxies. Astronomers utilize the fields of physics, chemistry, and mathematics in their studies.

The natural science divides into two branches: observational and theoretical astronomy. Observational astronomy analyzes information acquired from giving attention to the myriad of heavenly bodies. Theoretical astronomy uses analytical or numerical models to study the movement of celestial objects and evaluate various extraterrestrial events.

Physical cosmology, as a branch of theoretical astronomy, seeks to understand the origin, evolution, structure, and ultimate fate of the universe. It considers the entire makeup of outer space and the natural laws that keep it in order. Physical cosmology builds upon Albert Einstein's theory of general relativity. The use of radio telescopes and advances in astronomical observation techniques have aided in empirical verification of his formulations. As a science, physical cosmology measures and maps the cosmos, while developing current evolutionary theories of the universe.

There are three elements in the progression of creation: (1) the origin of the universe and stars (cosmological), (2) the origin and formation of the earth (geological), and (3) the origin and development of life on earth (biological). The reader should use the timeline at the end of this section as a reference when reviewing the remainder of the chapter. Figure 1 advances the idea that properly chosen biblical theology and physical cosmology can work cooperatively to bring a better understanding of the world.

The foremost comprehension of the Bible comes from an exegetical reading of the scriptures, where textual analysis leads to the correct interpretation. Additionally, the Christian's mandate to apply a proper theological construct of the Bible in relation to the world around them can be accomplished by placing appropriate levels of trust in the sciences to properly interpret the observable universe.

The timeline begins by placing the 13.8 billion-year-old universe of big bang cosmology in juxtaposition with the belief in old earth creationism. These views of science and religion find common ground by accepting the universe as being very old and seeing time have a beginning at the start of creation. Time initiates at "t = 0." The timeline then moves along to the present era by centering on the birth and final return of Jesus Christ.

Further synergy in science and religion is in the physical continuation of Earth and Venus after Christ's return. The solar evolution of our sun will continue in the main sequence phase beyond one billion years. Our planet becomes the final resting place for God's kingdom. The return of the heavenly armies brings paradise to Earth for the righteous, while Venus, as a lake of fire, can become the abode of the unrighteous.

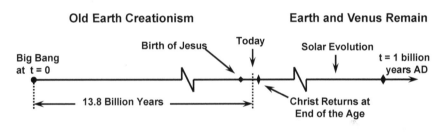

Figure 1
Biblical Theology in Accord with Physical Cosmology

Old Earth Creationism

As a recognized collection of Judeo-Christian texts, the Old Testament presents the creation story of the universe, planet Earth, and human civilization. Contained within the first two chapters of the book of Genesis are two similar accounts of creation. The first chapter presents a celestial focus of the creation, cementing humanity's purpose and place in the vastness of cosmic space. Beginning in Genesis 2:4b is the second creation story, which brings a terrestrial view to the creation. Each account gives direction to humans to sustain and replenish the earth. The texts are summarily concise in presenting the creation as the handiwork of an all-powerful God.

Biblical creationism is central to Christian theology and provides a critical perspective to understanding the origin and establishment of the known universe. Christian thinkers who consider the creation accounts in Genesis have developed two types of competing theologies: the first is young earth creationism and the second is old earth creationism. Both views consider God as the divine agent and causal force in making the world. In its basic formulation, however, only old earth creationism assimilates the findings of the sciences.

Young earth creationism has a long history in Judaism and Christianity, forming the basis for a traditional line of religious thought. The theology accepts a literal understanding of the Genesis narrative, arguing for a belief of the creation where each "day" (Heb. *yôm*) of the six-days of creation represents a 24-hour period. Young earth creationists also maintain that the earth is between 6000 and 10,000 years old. Young earth creationists do not accept findings in science that compete with a literal six-day creation period. As such, young earth creationism is in conflict with the big bang timeline.

One example exposing problems of young earth thinking is the speed of light in a vacuum ($c = 3 \times 10^8$ meters/sec). The universal physical constant is a fundamental aspect of the way space and time are unified in space-time. The term defines the maximum speed at which electromagnetic radiation (light) can travel in the universe. An elementary photon particle, which has no rest mass, can travel at the speed of light. Astronomers measure the distance to objects in the universe using the constant. The nearest galaxy, Andromeda, is 2.5 million light-years away. One light-year is about 6 trillion miles.

Young earth creationists would not have a sound explanation for why light from Andromeda takes 2.5 million years to travel to our eyes. Cosmic reality does not fit with the short timetable of young earth creationism. Some would claim that God set the light path in place for heavenly bodies during the six days of creation. The line of reasoning is an attempt to "superimpose the supernatural" on existing physical laws. Observing distant celestial objects is construed as a miraculous event, while ignoring the scientific facts. Playing the trump card of "supernatural" is an attempt to avoid theological discussion and to stymie science. The approach would not be necessary with a proper understanding of Scripture.

God establishes universal laws for human beings to appreciate, not as something to disregard with miracle solutions. Applying the thinking in a different arena, one might ask, "Do miracles define how God works in the hidden world of reproduction?" Our ancestors might have thought reproduction in the animal kingdom to be a miracle. Now, the biological processes of procreation have become fully understood. In the same manner, science has come to fully reveal God's truth about the age of the universe. Astronomy and astrophysics now understand the origin and workings of the cosmos. The fields should be looked upon with trust and even indebtedness.

At the same time, it is important to understand that existing physical laws do not lock out the possibility of miracles. Jehovah is not bound by the fabric of physical laws. God abides in them freely and habitually but can deviate at His choosing to intervene in the creation. For example, when Jesus gives sight to the blind or heals someone of leprosy, biological molecular structure reconfigures instantly. God receives the glory when miracles are placed in the proper context.

Old earth creationists argue for a different translation of the Hebrew word *yôm*, which can also mean "day-age" or "epoch." Beginning in Genesis 1:1, the interpretation transforms the meaning of *yôm* into boundless periods of time in the six day creation story. In Genesis 2:4b, which initiates the terrestrial story of creation, the word *yôm* speaks to eons of time for the formation of the heavens and the earth. These understanding bring juxtaposition between science and religion for the formation of the universe. Physical cosmology begins to make sense because it is in accord with the creation stories in Genesis.

Old earth creationism recognizes prevailing scientific evidence for the big bang expansion of the universe. It acknowledges solar system formation from a molecular cloud and the accretion of the planets. The theology accepts the established laws of physics, believing the light from distant galaxies took millions of years to reach Earth. Additionally, the basic ideas of geological science fit into the old earth creationism model, believing age-old forms of life can be found, accurately dated, and catalogued in the fossil record.

Thirteen billion years of time is incomprehensible to the average person, but it is not a consideration to a God who lives in eternity. Second Peter 3:8 reads "But do not ignore this one fact, beloved, that with the Lord one day is like a thousand years, and a thousand years are like one day." The Lord God, living in the eternal realm, embraces time in a way that goes beyond human comprehension. Scripture suggests that an extended timetable for creation does not have an effect on a divine being.

The important stellar activity of chemical development took billions of years to constitute the elements now recorded in the Cosmochemical Periodic Table of the Elements. When stars are born and then die, the process creates new elements. These elements are used in the formation of the next generation of stars, which contain more heavy metals. For example, the molecular cloud forming the structure of our sun has been augmented by the remains of many previous generations of stars. Examination and study in the field of stellar archeology continues. The goal of one research project is to populate stars into age categories using metallicity as the basis.[32]

---

32 The research is being conducted by scientists at the Massachusetts Institute of Technology. Locating and cataloguing stars according to metallicity creates a framework for understanding the chemical evolution of the cosmos. Curtis Brainard, "The Archeology of the Stars," *The New York Times: Science Times* (February 11, 2014), 1–2.

During the stellar development of chemical elements, the universe continued to expand. Several Bible verses throughout the Old Testament describing the heavens being "stretched out" by the Lord God correlate to the big bang theory of expansion.[33] In Jeremiah, the passages read, "It is he who made the earth by his power, who established the world by his wisdom, and by his understanding stretched out the heavens." The primitive Hebrew word *natah* in the passages means to "stretch out" or "extend." The heavens were not simply "set in place." The verses reinforce one another, and assist in relaying to readers the accurate idea about an expanding universe.

With respect to planetary development, old earth creationism accepts geological estimates for the age of the earth. The sun and the solar system are thought to have formed about 4.5 billion years ago through the discernible processes of star formation. The estimate for the timeline comes through modern techniques such as radiometric dating, which uses the known decay rate of a radioactive isotope. The planets in the solar system, fashioned around the same period as the sun, are a result of revolving matter gravitating together in the form of hot plasma from the molecular cloud.

Planets such as the earth form in size through the process of accretion and solidify from that point forward. The placement of the earth in the habitable zone of the solar system allows for the right planetary temperatures to facilitate the continuance of liquid water on the surface.[34] The origin of the terrestrial atmosphere is attributable to volcanic activity and the

---

33 The following passages contain reference to the heavens being stretched out: Job 9:8, Ps. 104:2, Isa. 42:5, Isa. 51:13, Jer. 10:12, Jer. 51:15 and Zech. 12:1. Coogan, *New Oxford Annotated Bible*, 736, 865, 1035, 1050, 1095, 1161, 1367 [Old Testament].

34 Scientists define the Circumstellar Habitable Zone (CHZ) of a terrestrial planet as the region around a star where liquid water can exist on the surface for extended periods. Guillermo Gonzalez and Jay W. Richards, *The Privileged Planet: How Our Place in the Cosmos Is Designed for Discovery* (Washington, DC: Regnery, 2004), 129.

outgassing of frozen or trapped material. The atmosphere assists in retaining water, an essential solvent having the ability to dissolve various compounds and to form essential solutions. The abundance of water around the globe facilitates carbon-based life. Carbon forms the key component for all naturally occurring life on Earth.

In terms of biological development, the scientific explanation of natural evolution lacks in convincing evidence. It remains a process by which time and chance can be applied to elemental mishmash and give rise to higher species. The linchpin for the mechanism is macroevolution, which is a theory centering on common descent. It is a hypothesis that feeds upon itself; that is, preconceived notions and foregone conclusions influence the analysis of observable data. The fossil record, which is often suggested to support macroevolution, does not, in reality, show a trace of any higher order transition.[35]

Faith-based scientists who adhere to old earth creationism address natural evolution using either progressive creationism or theistic evolution. Progressive creationism is a process where new types of living organisms form by divine intervention over advancing geological periods, in order to align with the day-ages of the Genesis story. The appearances of new life represent instances of direct intervention by Creator God.

During these epochs, various kinds of plants and animals appear in stages, with each stage lasting millions of years. The creation episodes are followed by periods of inactivity, where growth and dispersion of life forms occur. In harmony with Scripture and the archaeological record, progressive creationism maintains that species first appear in a fully formed state.

A good example of a Genesis day-age finds evidence in science during the geological period known as the Cambrian Explosion. In the centuries-old examination of the fossil record,

---

35 Reasons to Believe, *Does Macroevolution Fit the Fossil Record,* http:// www.reasons.org/ explore/topic/evolution (accessed May 20, 2014).

the Cambrian Explosion comes to surface as a significant era in creation. In paleontology, the Cambrian Explosion was the unparalleled emergence of organisms between 540 and 480 million years ago.[36] Characterizing the event was the sudden appearance of 25 to 35 major phyla.

The observation suggests that animals of incredible complexity appeared on the earth in a relatively short period of time without any evolutionary predecessors. Examination of fossil records indicates transitional fossils do not exist in the Cambrian Period, meaning no claim of primitive life forms evolving into higher life can be made. The episode suggests spontaneous creation by God, highly favoring the progressive creation model.

Progressive creationism is not compatible with macroevolution, which remains biologically indefensible and unsupported by the fossil record. However, microevolution, involving minor or mutational changes within a species, is affirmed as genetically sound. The process allows for environmental adaptation and survival. In terms of the origin of human beings, progressive creationism affirms direct involvement by the Creator. God is believed to have created Adam in His image in the last 10,000 to 150,000 years. The man was formed from the dust of the ground. He was followed by the woman Eve, taken from his rib.

The idea of theistic evolution is popular in some seminary circles. Theistic evolution accepts the big bang premise and early formation of the earth. It then envisions God using the process of natural evolution over hundreds of millions of years to create life forms, including human beings. The concept wreaks havoc on the historicity of Adam and Eve and the traditional

---

36 The Cambrian Explosion unleashed a plethora of complex organisms upon the earth. It is the most overwhelming biological event to have ever happened on the planet, paralleling the first formation of life itself. Peter D. Ward and Donald Brownlee, *Rare Earth: Why Complex Life is Uncommon in the Universe.* (New York: Copernicus Books, 2004), 131.

Christian view of human origin. Proponents contain the acts of God within the natural evolution process in developing the creation. Theistic evolution presents serious problems by subordinating the Word of God and casting doubt on the direct involvement of God as Creator.

The support for old earth and progressive creationism continues to grow, having taken a foothold in Christian thought. Understanding and accepting big bang cosmology, the truth about the age of the universe and the progressive concept of plant and animal creation does not give ground to naturalist thinking. Honoring the timeline for the age of the universe is simply agreeing with the evidence, acknowledging the facts and abiding in the physical laws that have been set in place by God. The teaching helps to avoid an intellectual schizophrenia, where scientific inquiry into cosmic formation feeds the mind Monday through Saturday, followed by faith in a literal six day creation attempting to take over on Sunday.

Old earth creationism assures the Bible can provide a reliable record of the creation story in alignment with the sciences, and as revealed through the inspiration of the writers. Humans are given the privilege, through the study of the Word, to explore and to fill in the details for understanding the human record on the earth. One takes comfort in knowing that life is in harmony because the scriptural record and the findings of sciences remain consistent.

Correlation between science and religion in the creation story leads to the unfolding of higher truth. Having truth is being in alignment with verified or indisputable fact. All truth is God's truth and results in one accord. The trustworthiness, the inspiration, the authority, and the power of Scripture in the light of correct theology will lead Christianity in truth. The sciences, given as a gift by God for understanding and safeguarding the earth, provide humanity with observable and verifiable truths. What is proven true in one field will ultimately hold true in the other. Contradictions do not exist at the summit of knowledge and wisdom, in the mind and thoughts of the Creator.

The Beginning of Time and *Creatio ex Nihilo*

For a major portion of human history, cosmology was not a well-understood subject. For lack of a telescope, the field was philosophical and metaphysical, with close ties to astrology and religion. Initially, the philosopher Plato expressed theories of the universe to explain the deeper realities of life. Unable to envision a rotating planet orbiting about the sun, it was Platonists who first began depicting a fixed Earth, centered in the cosmos and surrounded by celestial objects moving in circular motion. The ancient Greek worldview held great precedence, unable to be challenged until the seventeenth century.

Aristotle, renowned philosopher of classical antiquity and exemplar student of Plato, developed the three-dimensional spheres of geocentric thought, replacing the two-dimensional circles of Platonists. Rotating spheres transported the moon, sun, planets, and stars around a stationary earth. Using the Aristotelian model, Claudius Ptolemaeus logically assimilated a workable cosmology in AD 150. He attributed the order of spherical motion as being reflective of the divine.

In 1543 the proposal by Nicolas Copernicus ascribing orbiting motion to the earth, rather than the sun, was inconceivable. Yet this ground-breaking, heliocentric system would become the origin of scientific cosmology. The construction of a telescope and systematic exploration of the heavens by Galileo confirmed the Copernican model. Work by Johannes Kepler described the elliptical paths of planets. Sir Isaac Newton went on to formulate the laws of motion and universal gravitation, applying them to objects both on Earth and in the cosmos. His scientific thinking was to dominate ideas about physical cosmology for the next three centuries.

In terms of theories of cosmic structure, the early part of the twentieth century was embroiled in a debate between the views of a static or expanding universe. The 1900s began with the understanding of a static universe, where distant celestial bodies were deemed motionless. This belief ceased following an accumulation of credible measurements of shifting distant galaxies. Observation at the Lowell Observatory in Arizona in 1914 by Vesto Slipher brought forth a "drift hypothesis," where the Milky Way was in motion relative to other galaxies.

In 1927 Monsignor George Lemaître, a Belgian priest, astronomer, and professor of physics at the Catholic University of Louvain, published an obscure paper written in French documenting "red shift" in the cosmos. This phenomenon explains that the farther away a galaxy is, the greater the light is shifted toward the red portion of the electromagnetic spectrum.[37] Red is at the lower end of the frequency spectrum where the wavelength widens out, suggesting an opening up of stellar space. The discovery was the first to give support for a stretching or enlarging universe.

Paralleling Lemaître's work in Europe, American astronomer Edwin Hubble published a paper in 1929 demonstrating a linear velocity-distance relationship in observed spiral nebulae. The work was accomplished using the same red shift phenomenon, and has become known as Hubble's law or Lemaître's law. The findings reveal that the farther away a galaxy is from the earth, the greater the recessional velocity. The idea of galaxy speeds increasing with increasing distance gave further evidence for an expanding universe.

A second issue of debate during the twentieth century was whether or not the expanding universe was in a steady state condition, or if the cosmos had an origin or single point source. The steady state theory envisions a universe that has

---

37 The electromagnetic spectrum encompasses all possible frequencies of radiation in the universe. The eight classes of radiation include gamma, x-ray, ultraviolet, visible, infrared, terahertz, microwave and radio waves.

always existed and continues to expand, with no beginning of time. The model envisions a continuously homogeneous and uniform distribution of old and new objects in the sky, as galaxies emerge within the expanding space.

In 1931, Lemaître countered the notion of a steady state, officially proposing a theory for the universe having a finite beginning as a "single quantum." The single quantum refers to the start of the universe in an initial or gravitational singularity state.[38] In 1949, the theory was coined "big bang." The paradigm shift would lead to the concept of a beginning to time in the universe. The new physical cosmology attracted the attention of world leaders. Pope Pius XII announced in 1952 that the big bang was in harmony with the Bible because it affirms the notion of a transcendent Creator.

The discovery of cosmic microwave background radiation (CMBR) in the latter half of the twentieth century solidified the theory among scientists. CMBR finds its source in the big bang expansion. As a result, the big bang became the accepted standard of the scientific community. And with the paradigm came the arrival of an alignment between biblical theology and physical cosmology.

The first line of Genesis states, "In the beginning when God created the heavens and the earth ..." In probing deeper into the statement, one can ask, "In the beginning of what?" with the appropriate response being, "in the beginning of time." The physical universe has not always existed but had a beginning, along with time itself. While in His eternal sphere of influence, God was actively assessing His forthcoming universe before the beginning of time. Scripture notes the Almighty's consideration and planning for human beings before the ages and before

---

38 The initial or gravitational singularity of infinite density contained all of the mass, energy and space-time in the universe. The rapid expansion of the big bang facilitates the creation of the present-day universe.

the foundation of the world.[39] In the eternal realm preceding time, God measured and thought through His purpose for humankind.

So, where does time come from? Time (t) is a created dimension of the universe, as were matter and space. Time is fashioned in association with, or as a derivative of, the eternal realm. Eternity is the domain wherein God exists. Eternity is not a place of timelessness (without time), but rather a time-integrated state without beginning or end.[40] The Almighty selected an aspect of the eternal realm for the creation of time. In the temporal realm, time has a start or a beginning at t = 0.

The big bang is the event identifying the creation of time, space, and matter. Contained in an initial or gravitational singularity, the compacted point is thought to have contained all of the mass-energy of the universe. It is at t = 0 where the big bang expansion begins.[41] At the incipient stage of creation, all matter would have been in a highly compressed or incalculably dense state. The expansion of the matter caused a cooling effect, leading to the formation of subatomic particles that eventually became the building blocks for hydrogen and helium.

In theology, the common Latin expression *creatio ex nihilo* means "creation out of nothing." The phrase applies to the formation of original matter in the universe at the beginning of time. Science has no explanation for the origination of matter

---

39 In 1 Cor. 2:7; Eph. 1:4; 2 Tim. 1:9; Titus 1:2; and 1 Pet. 1:20, one notes the phrases "before the ages began" and "before the foundations of the world," Coogan, *New Oxford Annotated Bible*, 271, 321, 358, 363, 396 [New Testament].

40 Eternity is not endless ordinary time. Neither is eternity an aggregate of all events into a single, timeless, unstructured present. Eternity is a differentiating unity called co-presence, which has a "past-present-future" makeup. The structure has no beginning or end, holding the history of all events in the universe together. Robert John Russell, *Time in Eternity: Pannenberg, Physics and Eschatology in Creative Mutual Interaction* (Notre Dame, IN: University of Notre Dame Press, 2012), 13–14.

41 Robert John Russell, *Cosmology: From Alpha to Omega* (Minneapolis, MN: Fortress Press, 2008), 77.

and energy for the initial singularity of the big bang expansion. However, biblical theology can provide a solution. The original matter for the big bang expansion came from God and was created by God from nothing. God did not create this matter from His own being or spiritual essence. The substance is separate from God and was made for use in forming His creation.

In science, one can define "nothing" three ways: (1) the absence of matter, (2) the absence of matter and energy, or most importantly, (3) the absence of matter, energy and space. The big bang expansion from the initial singularity created matter, energy, and space. The physical space of outer space did not exist before the big bang event. Matter and energy formed newly created physical space through expansion, which became the spatial universe. In the same manner, the biblical notion of *creatio ex nihilo* means the absence of matter, energy, and space.

Christian tradition cites Genesis 1:1 and the supporting text of Saint Augustine of Hippo to give credence to the idea of time and matter being created out of nothing. In Augustine's *Confessions*, the philosopher and theologian states,

> In the beginning, that is from yourself, in your wisdom which is begotten of your substance, you made something and made it out of nothing. For you made heaven and earth not out of your own self, or it would be equal to your only-begotten Son and therefore to yourself ... That is why you made heaven and earth out of nothing, a great thing and a little thing, since you, both omnipotent and good, make all things good, a great heaven and a little earth.[42]

---

42 Augustine sees the heavens belonging to God and the earth given to the sons of all people. Henry Chadwick, trans., *Saint Augustine Confessions* (New York: Oxford University Press, 1998), 249.

For Augustine, *creatio ex nihilo* includes the time domain.[43] With the initial creation event, time came into existence and matter was set in motion. Simultaneously, the dispersion of the matter creates physical space that previously did not exist. The increase of time and space are concurrent with expanding matter. Therefore, one understands the creation of the universe to begin as an initial singularity, using matter and energy created *ex nihilo*, which beginning at t = 0 expands to create space. The interdisciplinary confluence of physical cosmology and biblical creationism makes a declaration through which God calls the universe into being.

The confines of planet Earth dictate every person encounter space and time as dimensions detached from one another. Daily living necessitates space and time being separate entities that remain unmodified or "absolute" in basic construct. Analog and digital clocks, smart phones, watches, calendars and planning schedules draw our attention to an absolute time that is split-off from the substance of the planet. One views people, places and open spaces in the physical world as articles separate from time.

Physical cosmology views the dimensions interactively. In the study of the cosmos, astrophysicists demonstrate time, space, and matter to be connected to one another. The physical laws of the universe dictate a new reality. The notion of space and time becomes space-time, with measurements always considered relative to the observer's position.

The interrelationship of time, space, and matter finds expression in the 1905 theory of special relativity. Published by Albert Einstein, the theory shows the accepted physical relationship between space and time, while placing limits on the Newtonian idea of absolute space and time. The equation

---

43 Ted Peters, "On Creating the Cosmos," in *Physics, Philosophy and Theology: A Common Quest for Understanding*, ed. Robert John Russell; William R. Stoeger, SJ; and George V. Coyre, SJ (Vatican City State: Vatican Observatory Publications, 1988), 279.

$E = mc^2$ became a formulation of special relativity, showing not only how matter and energy interrelate, but also defining a curvature to space-time.[44] The postulate applies to all inertial (nonaccelerating) frames of reference, asserting that the speed of light remains constant regardless of the relative motion of the light source.

Frames of reference are a way of stating that the laws of physics should be the same for all observers, regardless of how they are moving through space. Following the publication of special relativity, Einstein began working on how to incorporate gravity into his relativistic modeling. In 1915, he issued the theory of general relativity, which provides a unified description of gravity as a geometric property of space and time. It extends the concept of special relativity by taking gravitational acceleration into account in reference frames.

The idea of a space-time continuum was already in existence, but under general relativity, Einstein was able to describe gravity as the geometric bending of space-time. The crucial aspects of the theory are written using a system of partial differential equations. The field equations describe the curvature of space-time and the distribution of matter through space-time. The effect of matter and space-time on each other is what is normally perceived as gravity.

In later years, British astrophysicists Stephen Hawking, Roger Penrose, and George Ellis did important work to solve the equations of general relativity. In 1965, Penrose gave credence to the notion of a singularity being contained within a black hole region of space and that a given body under gravitational collapse must eventually form a singularity.

---

44 The mass-energy equivalence formula $E = mc^2$ expresses energy (E) as a function of mass (m) times the squaring of the speed of light in a vacuum (c). The equation has use in understanding the great amount of energy released during nuclear fission reactions (e.g., in nuclear reactors and atomic weapons). Graphically representing the speed of light (c^2 factor) can demonstrate the curved path an object takes while traveling through space-time.

In 1968, Hawking and Ellis published a joint paper indicating the certainty of past convergences of light-like and time-like "geodesics" in the cosmos.[45] In general relativity, a geodesic, the shortest line between two points on a curved surface, generalizes the notion of a straight line to curved space-time. In 1970, a joint paper published by Hawking and Penrose reaffirmed the idea of convergence in a past light cone.[46] The idea of *light convergence* in these papers showed that space and time must have an origin or meeting point concurrent with that of matter and energy.

A geometric depiction for Einstein's theory of special relativity can be made using a space-time plot. Scientists can visualize or represent space and time events graphically using the image of light cones. In theoretical physics, past and future light cones work to form a manifold representative path that a light source radiating in all directions would take through space-time.

Space-time plotting can be visualized in three dimensions if two axes are chosen to be *spatial* dimensions and the third axis is the *time-like* dimension. Shown in figure 2 is a 3-D graphic of a past and future light cone used by physicists to extrapolate present event (A).[47] Time is shown along one axis, but is being treated as a spatial dimension in the light cone formulation. Adding the remaining third space dimension would form the complete four-dimensional (4-D) representation of

---

45 Stephen W. Hawking and George F. R. Ellis, "The Cosmic Black-Body Radiation and the Existence of Singularities in Our Universe," *Astrophysical Journal*, 152 (1968): 25–36.

46 Stephen Hawking and Roger Penrose, "The Singularities of Gravitational Collapse and Cosmology," *Proceedings of the Royal Society of London*, Series A 314 (1970): 529–548.

47 In mathematical physics, the representation is known as Minkowski space-time. One can draw a parallel notion to Euclidean space, which is 2-D for a plane or 3-D for a three-dimensional space. The Cartesian coordinate system defines Euclidean space. The x-axis, y-axis, and z-axis are the three lines that create the coordinate plane, meeting at the origin.

space-time. In 4-D space, the conical circles below would form into spheres.

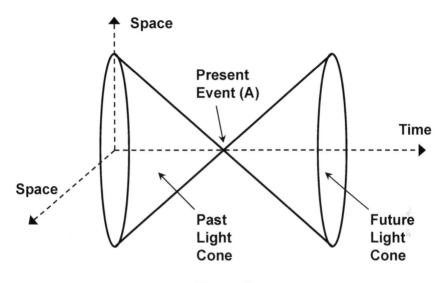

Figure 2
Past and Future Light Cones

Following the past light cone from present event A, the light spreads out to greater distances as the cone area increases. In traveling back in the universe, the light path becomes bent by space-time. The pictorial would change to make the straight lines of the past light cone hyperbolic or curved in shape. If there is sufficient material substance in the cosmos, the light ray dispersion will reach a maximum and then begin converging due to gravitational effects. The 1970 Hawking-Penrose publication mathematically addresses the reality of light cone convergence. An adequate amount of matter existing in the universe will refocus the light. The light convergence toward the big bang singularity points to the universe having a beginning in time.[48]

The question arises as to whether or not there is sufficient

48 Stephen W. Hawking, *A Brief History of Time* (New York: Bantam Books, 1998), 53.

particle substance in the universe to focus the past light cone. When observing the night sky using the naked eye or a telescope, one peers into the apparent emptiness of interplanetary, interstellar, and intergalactic space. The dark vacuum of space, however, is not a perfect vacuum. The visual notion of nothingness is a partial assessment because the human eye and the optical instruments that aid the eye function primarily in the visible portion of the electromagnetic spectrum. In order to be comprehensive, one needs to examine the plasma of space.

In 1964, the discovery of cosmic microwave background radiation (CMBR) unveiled vast amounts of thermal radiation in the universe. Scientists Robert Wilson and Arno Penzias were testing a sensitive antenna designed to detect low levels of microwave radiation when they picked up on CMBR. The low amount of microwave radiation was like noise in their test system setup. The disturbance is akin to an electrical problem on a television screen, which visually appears as "snow." The scientists concluded that the perturbation was coming from outer space. Moving the antenna around did not help matters; the noise signal was arriving at the same level from all directions in space.

What is CMBR; that is to say, of what is it composed? Essentially, CMBR is a type of radiation or energy in the form of charged particles. Ionized hydrogen and other high-energy subatomic particles fill the universe in every direction with thermal radiation or heat. The black-body radiation measures at 3° Kelvin, the temperature to which the universe has cooled. In order for energy to be so evenly distributed, the scattering must have taken billions of years.

Considering these findings, scientists deduce CMBR to be the remains of radiant heat from the big bang event. The idea of remnant heat from a sudden expansion was to end speculation of a steady state universe. The blanket of uniform, energized, atomic, and subatomic particles brings electromagnetic opacity to the universe. The opacity demonstrates there is significant matter in the universe to refocus the past light cone and draw conclusions for an initial singularity and a beginning of time.

In referencing Figure 1, the depiction is of big bang cosmology being in accord with biblical theology over time. Genesis 1:1 gives witness to time having a beginning, and to the creation of "the heavens [space-time, energy] and the earth [matter]." In like kind, the field of astrophysics, utilizing general relativity principles during the last century, deduced a beginning to time, along with matter, energy and space. An important agreement is now realized between science and religion – the inception of time. Future study could reveal more relationships.

In terms of ongoing research, cosmology looks to accurately measure the effects of dark matter and dark energy. The invisible components are labeled dark, not because of a lack of understanding, but because the findings do not emit light. The detection of dark matter comes through the gravitational influence it has on visible matter. Dark matter constitutes 25% of the mass-energy of the universe. Dark energy represents 70% of the mass-energy of the universe. These discoveries give reason for additional research to determine their properties. Understanding the new types of matter and energy is part of the challenge of exploring the evolution and ultimate fate of the universe.

Earth and Venus Remain

In terms of the formation of the universe, physical cosmology and old earth creationism share an extended timeline. The expanding universe is 13.8 billion years old and continues to age. But what does the future of the cosmic creation look like? What does the coming of the kingdom of God to the planet have in store for the universe? Does heaven on Earth and Venus as the lake of fire correspond with the expected longevity of the solar system? Astrophysicists see the solar system and planets remaining healthy for a significant length of time in the Milky Way spiral. The assertion of a bright galactic future bodes well for further collaboration between faith and science.

In the book *Global Catastrophic Risks*, editor Nick Bostrom addresses a number of the gravest risks facing humanity in the twenty-first century. As the director of the Future of Humanity Institute at Oxford University, Bostrom performs extensive research into the probability of natural disasters or human-induced catastrophies unfolding over time. In evaluating cosmic concerns, he notes an interesting, even distinctive, point about celestial processes. The astronomical parameters predicting the long-term health of the universe can be measured with high precison. This greatly increases the degree of certainty to being able to predict the future of the universe.[49]

We begin by examining the hypotheses for the ultimate fate of the universe. The power working to cause an expansion of the universe is called the cosmological constant. The force is the simplest grasp of dark energy. Opposing the force of expansion is gravitational effects. Gravity and mass/energy compete against each other to form either an open, closed, or flat universe. Depending on the quantity of mass/energy, the universe has three different futures:

1. Open—There is sufficient mass/energy for gravity not to be able to halt the expansion, so the universe expands forever.
2. Flat—There is just enough mass/energy to keep gravity at bay and continue the expansion, making for an open universe.

---

49 The projections are based on the current understanding of dark energy in the universe and the existing laws of physics and astronomy. Increasing scientific knowledge could result in a revision to the estimates. Nick Bostrom and Milan M. Cirkovic, eds., *Global Catastrophic Risks,* (New York: Oxford University Press, 2008), 33–34.

3. Closed—There is insufficient mass/energy, so gravity can halt the expansion. The universe will eventually collapse back to a singularity.

In examining the cosmological parameters, scientists see evidence for an open-model universe that will expand forever. Theoretically, an expanding universe will experience increasing entropy, leading to a state of thermal equilibrium that is unable to support life. Stellar evolution and star formation will eventually come to a close at some future point. Some estimates see the universe being 100 trillion years old when stars finally stop shining.[50] The long-term health of the universe allows events closer to home to play out.

One scenario for planetary problems appears in the intergalactic collision of the Milky Way with the large, spiral-shaped galaxy of Andromeda. The celestial body is 2.5 million light-years away and moving rapidly in our direction, with estimated contact in 3 to 4 billion years. The interaction of the two spiral galaxies is likely to create a merger, with little chance of star collision. The additional stars in the galactic merger will lead to a night sky that is twice the current brightness.[51] The likelihood of disruption for our sun and planetary system is very low, but scientists speculate the unified assembly of stars will sweep our solar system to a point farther from the galactic center.

Another extraterrestrial risk is from the impact of a large asteroid or comet. The lethality of a collision depends on the size, velocity, composition, and angle of incidence of the meteorite and whether the impact is on land or water. An asteroid strike on Mexico's Yucatán Peninsula 65 million years ago is thought to have caused the mass extinction of plant and animal species. The event led to the disappearance of nonavian dinosaurs. The width of the Chicxulub crater is more

---

50 Ibid., 39.
51 Ibid., 37.

than 100 miles, which calculates back to an incoming meteorite diameter of more than 5 ½ miles.

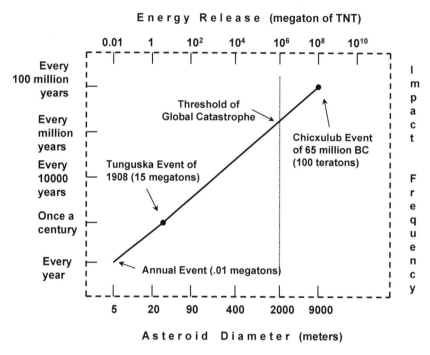

Figure 3
The Geological Record of Impact on Earth

The graph above incorporates a timeline showing that the earth rarely experiences a large-size asteroid strike.[52] Asteroids enter the atmosphere every day, but seldom does one reach the ground. The critical threshold for a world-wide catastrophe is in the 1- to 1.2-mile range. At this diameter or larger, dust in the atmosphere could circle the globe and temporarily reduce

---

52 Two celestial events plotted over geological time create a linear historical record of impact. The first point is the prehistoric Chicxulub impact at the tip of the Yucatán Peninsula. The second point is the 1908 Tunguska event in a remote part of Siberia. Analysis of samples spread over an 800 square mile area indicates a comet or asteroid burst in the air prior to impact. Astr 1210 (O'Connell) Study Guide, "Impacts and Bio-Extinctions," http://www. astro.virginia.edu/class/ oconnell/astr121/im/asteroid-impact-frequency-NASA.gif (accessed July 27, 2014).

sunlight for plant growth. Burning embers falling from the blast could ignite fires in multiple locations. If the meteorite struck water, a tsunami of large-scale proportions would hit the shores of many countries. The consequences of the collision, however, would not eliminate intelligent life around the globe.

Ultimately, the fate of the planets in the solar system lies in the hands of a gradually warming sun. Classified as a G-type main sequence star, the sun has not changed significantly since reaching the phase shortly after formation 4.5 billion years ago. The sun generates energy by the nuclear fusion of hydrogen to helium. As the process continues, the sun will grow brighter and larger.

In about 2 billion years, the seas of Earth will evaporate from the increase in temperature. The end of complex life will come sooner, probably in 1 to 1.5 billion years due to the buildup of heat. In 5 billion years, the sun will increase in size to a red giant. The diameter will be large enough to consume Mercury, Venus, and possibly Earth, as measured by their current orbits.

The aft-mentioned number of 1 to 2 billion years boundlessly exceeds the lifespan of the average individual. The length of time since the initial recording of history has only been about 5000 years. The totality of the human experience on the planet is fractional, even minute, compared to the billion-plus years that lie ahead for the planet and solar system. The stellar evolutionary process of our sun provides planets such as Earth and Venus with the opportunity to be around for a very long time.

What are the biblical prognostications for the future of the universe, the solar system, and the planets? Do any of these views maintain harmony with science? Several scriptures in the Bible help to inform us of end-time prophecies addressing heaven and the earth.

A theme known as the "Day of the Lord" is found in both Testaments. The Day of the Lord is a time of God's personal intervention in human affairs. The Old Testament prophets use the term for that time when the God of Israel intervenes in history, with the intent of either judging or restoring the nation. In the New Testament, the phrase refers to the Lord's Second Coming. In first Thessalonians 5:2, Paul tells the church "that the day of the Lord will come like a thief in the night," in order to catch by surprise those who are ill-equipped.

The scenario for the Day of the Lord depends on how one interprets eschatological events in the Bible. The occasion can occur either at the beginning, middle, or end of the seven year of tribulation. In all cases, the apocalyptic event wraps up the dispensation of the present church age. If the timing is before or during the seven years of hardship, a physical rapture occurs where the material body of the believer is removed from the earth.[53] If the Day of the Lord happens at the end of the tribulation period, then it combines with the Second Coming of Christ to create a resurrection-rapture.

The Second Coming is commonly referred to as the Second Advent or *Parousia*, a Greek word meaning arrival or presence. In discussing end-time events with His disciples, Jesus states in Matthew 24:30 that all the people of the earth "will see the Son of Man coming on the clouds of heaven with power and great glory." Revelation 19:11–16 describes Christ's return on a white horse. The rider is called Faithful and True. The Lord of glory will come down out of heaven with His armies to defeat the enemy and rule the nations.

People of faith await the return of Christ to set up His kingdom on the earth. It is a biblical mandate to be ready for the Lord's appearing. Attention to eschatology produces much excitement in Christianity, due to the prophetic and

---

53 Support cited for the rapture is in 1 Thessalonians 4:16–7. The passage reads, "For the Lord himself, with a cry of command, with the archangel's call and with the sound of God's trumpet, will descend from heaven, and the dead in Christ will rise first. Then we who are alive, who are left, will be caught up in the clouds together with them to meet the Lord in the air; and so we will be with the Lord forever." Coogan, *New Oxford Annotated Bible*, 343 [New Testament]

potentially imminent nature of the Second Advent. A great deal of Christian literature and television evangelism address apocalyptic scenarios, anticipating the Lord's return. Some evaluate current news trends in the anticipation of seeing end-time activities unfold.

Bible prophecy regarding the Second Coming of Christ reveals two contrasting views for the fate of the planet. The first scenario pictures a physical termination to our terrestrial world. The planets, the solar system, the Milky Way galaxy, and the remaining heavens are thought to disappear as well. It is a cataclysmic finish to what is familiar to the eye, in order to establish the heavenly kingdom. The theology espouses an "end of the world" approach, where little, if any, familiarity with our time-honored planet and sky remain. It is one interpretation of the new heaven and the new earth (Rev. 21:1).

The second end-time approach acknowledges a continuation of the planet. The new heaven and new earth is not a cosmic re-creation, but a revitalizing and cleansing of the earth and firmament. The result is a safeguarding and preservation of our material environment after the Lord's return. The theology acknowledges an "end to the age" approach. It views the new heaven and the new earth as undergoing a renewing or refreshing. Preservation of the fabric of the earth, the surrounding firmament, and the universe at-large plays a key ingredient in the formation of an eternal paradise for all to enjoy.

The first "end of the world" concept brings God and the eternal kingdom down from the firmament, while simultaneously eradicating the earthly environment. Bible teachers heralding this view consider the planet to disappear entirely as the heavenly throne descends into the atmosphere. Apparently, the presence of God the Father is more than the earth can handle. Depending on the adaptation, the solar system, the Milky Way galaxy, and the entire universe fold up as well, ushering in God's unimaginable paradise.

This type of prediction finds a place in books such as, *The Popular Encyclopedia of Biblical Prophecy*, coedited by Tim LaHaye, creator and coauthor of the Left Behind series. The encyclopedia provides extensive material concerning the end-times. The appearance of Christ and the heavenly armies is made out to be an earth-shattering event. According to the text, "In the presence of this divine majesty, the earth and its immediate atmosphere vanish."[54] The end of the world scenario has the firmament and our time-honored planet disappearing completely. Any semblance of previous scientific understanding of the cosmos has come to a close.

The eschatology does not take the whole of Scripture into consideration. The bulk of the interpretation seems to anchor on one lone verse, which is not convincing in the overall context. In 2 Peter 3:10 we read, "But the day of the Lord will come like a thief, and then the heavens will pass away with a loud noise, and the elements will be dissolved with fire, and the earth and everything that is done on it will be disclosed."

This passage presents contextual difficulty when examining the previous verses. In 2 Peter 3:6–7, the apostle recounts Noah's flood and states that by the same word, "the present heavens and earth have been reserved for fire." The result of the flood, however, did not destroy the earth. There was the preservation of a renewable environment after the flood.

Second, the book of Revelation provides no record of a global fire destroying the fabric of the planet after the return of the Lord (Rev. 19:11–16). The physical earth remains, as evidenced by the holy city, the New Jerusalem, coming down out of heaven (Rev. 21:2) and God willingly makes his home among mortals (Rev. 21:3). The word mortal translates from the Greek word *anthropos*, meaning man-faced or human being. The human creature can only dwell in a specially kept environment like the planet Earth.

---

54 Tim LaHaye and Ed Hinson, eds., *The Popular Encyclopedia of Bible Prophecy*, (Eugene, OR: Harvest House, 2004), 126.

Third, the 2 Peter 3:10 verse lacks a scriptural cross-reference. The idea of using scripture to interpret scripture is a common theme in many hermeneutic approaches. In searching out "the heavens will pass away with a loud noise," one cannot find a suitable cross-reference to assist in understanding the phrase. The passage becomes challenging to understand. Its use as the cornerstone for an "end of the world" eschatology becomes cause for concern.

The catastrophic end of the world scenario envisioned by some Bible scholars is presumptuous. God has no requirement set in place for universal cataclysmic destruction, in order to bring His saints to a paradisiacal environment. There is not a pressing purpose for the heavens and the earth to suddenly disappear at the Second Coming of Christ. Caution, even skepticism, about accepting an "end to the world" is advisable to everyone, and especially to those who study the word of God.

Similar to young earth creationism, the biblically conceived end of the world view attempts to bypass natural laws and "superimpose the supernatural" on the cosmic order. Interestingly, both theological approaches are often presented in one evangelical package as a warning against idolatry.[55] It is somehow honoring to God for those of faith to chop off the back end and the front end of the figure 1 timeline. On the contrary, assimilating reality is best done when individuals consider both the scriptures and scientific facts about past and potentially future events. Science and religion work together to reveal higher truth for a lasting continuance to the physical world and cosmos.

The wisdom of the prophetic voice triumphs when

---

55 The Bible-answering website GotQuestions.org uses the sin of idolatry as the reason for needing to accept the short timetable for creation and the sudden end to the world. Bible believers are thought to worship humankind and the power of science when giving credence to what physical cosmology teaches. GotQuestions.org, *What are Some Modern Forms of Idolatry?*, http://www.gotquestions.org/idolatry-modern.html (accessed July 22, 2014).

recognizing a prolongation to the order of terrestrial living when the kingdom of God comes to fruition on Earth. Aligning with this theological thought requires an "end of the age," rather than an "end of the world" perspective. The recording of history comes through the earmarking of end of the age episodes, where certain realities of life are present until a transition occurs. Following the transition, new lifestyles, pursuits and preferences become present in the world.

The three divisions of Western history divide into Classical Antiquity, the Middle Ages, and the Modern Era. The Middle Ages, or medieval period, provide a bridge between the ancient world and the modern world. The historical period began in the fifth century with the fall of the Roman Empire. One of the highlights of the era was the isolation of Europe from the rest of the known world, resulting in a society lax in general awareness, where superstition rather than perception ruled the thought life. The printing press, as a means for disseminating information, had not come into being.

The changeover from the medieval period to the modern era brought an occasion for the end of the age. The dawn of the new era came in the fifteenth century with the Renaissance, a long and complex cultural development permanently affecting European life. Further maturation and enrichment would follow during the Enlightenment. These movements had dramatic effects on the sciences, religious thought, fine arts, literature, architecture, music, dance, and philosophy. Because lives and lifestyles revolutionized, and then continued in a new construct, the phrase "end of the age" applies to the transition.

The Bible presents a spiritual end of the age example in the first advent or incarnation of Christ. The Bible tells the reader, "He was destined before the foundation of the world, but was revealed at the end of the ages for your sake" (1 Pet. 1:20). The life, death, and resurrection of Jesus Christ made an indelible mark in human history two thousand years ago. God's revelation of Himself through the Son brought fulfillment to Old Testament scriptures and paved the way for spiritual understanding and right relationship. God's mercy, grace, and forgiveness offered through the cross brought the beginning of a new age. The perception of God changes dramatically in the New Testament. As a result, lives, hearts, and thinking processes altered throughout the known world.

A similar "end of the age" scenario pertains to the Second Advent. The appearing of Jesus will occur at the end of the modern era, ushering in sweeping changes around the globe. His arrival will be instantaneous and worldwide; visible to everyone living on the earth at the time. God's sovereign rule will be on the familiar territory of a completely renewed planet Earth.

This second eschatological view detailing the Second Coming of Christ brings the end of the age, but not the physical termination of the planet, the solar system, or the universe at large. The reasoning sees the celestial paradise of heaven coming down to the earth, while preserving a renewed planet and surrounding atmosphere. The new heaven and the new earth will be a familiar material environment, where resurrected and immortal beings can enjoy family, friends, animals, and the presence of God.

The Bible addresses the idea of the earth being a never-ending terrestrial world in both Testaments. The following seven passages provide suitable cross-reference to one another, which reinforce the underlying concept. Scriptural consistency assures the reader of the correct interpretation of an ongoing planet.

> Psalm 37:29—The righteous shall inherit the land, and live in it forever.

> Psalm 104:5—You set the earth on its foundations, so that it shall never be shaken.

Ecclesiastes 1:4—A generation goes, and a generation comes, but the earth remains forever.

Matthew 5:5—Blessed are the meek, for they will inherit the earth.

Matthew 6:10—Your kingdom come, your will be done, on earth as it is in heaven (the Lord's Prayer).

Matthew 25:34—Then the king will say to those at his right hand, Come, you that are blessed by my Father, inherit the kingdom prepared for you from the foundation of the world.

Revelation 5:10—You have made them to be a kingdom of priests serving our God, and they will reign on earth.

The verse in Matthew 5:5 is taken from the Beatitudes. The Beatitudes are declarations of blessedness made by Jesus in the beginning of the Sermon on the Mount. The blessed individuals are those who attain salvation. In these passages, the Lord is giving assurance about the future kingdom of God coming to the earth. In the passage, Jesus pledges that His people will acquire this planetary domain for being meek. A meek person has a calm temperament that is not easily provoked.

Matthew 6:10 is part of the Lord's Prayer or "Our Father," which Jesus taught as the model prayer to his disciples. It is the central petition of Christianity, having been fully appropriated into church liturgy over the centuries and repeated innumerable times in the devotional life of the faithful. The prayer begins with the address, *"Our Father in heaven, hallowed be your name"* and continues with 6:10: *"Your kingdom come, your will be done, on earth as it is in heaven."* In the verse, one prays both for God's kingdom to come to Earth and for God's will to be done on Earth. When the faithful utter this prayer, God is hearing a request for His kingdom to come to our home planet.

Jesus speaks to the consummation of the age, rather than the end of the world, in the Great Commission of Matthew 28:16–20. The passage formulates the basic principles of Christian service by emphasizing baptism, ministry, missionary work, and evangelism. In his final remark in Matthew 28:20, Jesus assures the disciples that he is always with them, even to the end of the age. The NRSV translates the Greek *sunteleías toú aioónós* as "end of the age." The KJV initially translated the passage as "end of the world" but provides an update in the NKJV to say "end of the age." *Aioónós* properly translates as "age" and not as "world."

The Gloria Patri (Glory Be to the Father) is a short hymn of praise seen in Roman Catholic, Anglican, and Eastern Orthodox liturgies. The familiar version used in the North American liturgical readings recites as follows, *"Glory to the Father, and to the Son, and to the Holy Spirit. As it was in the beginning, is now, and ever shall be, world without end. Amen."* The world without end is a reference to the continuation of life on Earth at the end of the ages.

Using an "end of the age" approach continues the accord in Figure 1 between big bang cosmology and biblical old earth creationism. A key aspect of the kingdom of God's return is that the universe remains fundamentally unchanged. The idea portrays Earth as a future place of peace and happiness, while maintaining Venus as a place of loss and sadness. The theological approach provides for the continuation of the sun, planets, natural satellites and all objects in the solar system. Christ's return to establish sovereign rule on the earth preserves physical cosmology, providing harmony between religion and science with respect to the future of the cosmos.

The previous chapter presents the final judgment scene, where books open before the throne to review the lives of the resurrected dead. Having come up out of Hades, each inhabitant will have to give an account of his or her life. If the name of the individual is not written in the book of life, departure from the Lord's presence and the pleasant surroundings of the new earth is necessary. The paradisiacal planet will not be home to those who have been found guilty. These people must depart from the glory of God and His beautifully restored world. Regrettably, they will be lifted off the ground, guided into interplanetary space, and brought to a soft landing on a planet such as Venus.

The soul and the immortal spiritual body have physical mass, so they can be bound by gravity to any world. The specifics of the claim will be addressed in the next chapter. Immortal spiritual bodies are quite durable, being able to easily survive in harsh terrestrial locations. Like the resurrected body of Jesus, displaced spiritual beings will have phenomenal capabilities and be able to interact with the material environment.

An open question remains concerning the eschatological picture. Eternal life is a declaration used many times in Scripture to accompany the gift of salvation. The idea of forever, however, does not reconcile with solar evolution. The sun will become a red giant and engulf the orbit of Earth in five billion years. From an eternal perspective, the situation is less than permanent.

In a future eon, God may take steps because the sun cycle brings a natural close to the solar system. This writing does not answer how or when God, living in His eternal kingdom on Earth, will work to address the stellar evolution of the sun. One point can be made clear. The sphere of the maturing universe, where various cosmic issues tend to arise, is the proper domain wherein God can be expected to act and to provide satisfactory resolution.

CHAPTER 4

Satan and the Eternal Soul

But the wicked will be cut off from the earth,
And the unfaithful will be uprooted from it. (NKJV)

Proverbs 2:22

Satan and Fallen Angels

Who is Satan? The Bible restricts the most investigative reader to scattered references and incidental encounters. Establishing a complete understanding of Satan and his operative mode in the spiritual domain of darkness is not easy. Yet in piecing the particulars together, a picture unfolds of a high-ranking angelic being with a malicious attitude. Fallen from good-standing and prominence with God, this notorious figure led a host of lower-ranking angels in an enormous spiritual mutiny before the fall of humanity. In Scripture, his portrayal is as a rebellious, vindictive spirit who despises God and contends with His holy angels (Jude 1:9, Rev. 12:7).

Satan is synonymous with the devil. His nature is one of complete depravity. He is extremely self-absorbed and deceitful, willingly telling lies at every opportunity. His first appearance in

Scripture is as the serpent in the Garden of Eden. Ever working to destroy all that is good, he manages to tempt Adam and Eve into disobedience. In response to the fall, the Lord God tells the serpent in Genesis 3:15, "I will put enmity between you and the woman, and between your offspring and hers; he will strike your head, and you will strike his heel." Since that time, Satan has been the adversary of all peoples.

One understands Satan having full access to wander the planet or enter into the celestial heaven. In Job 1:6–7, the narrator tells the reader, "One day the heavenly beings came to present themselves before the Lord, and Satan also came among them. The Lord said to Satan, 'Where have you come from?' Satan answered the Lord, 'From going to and fro on the earth, and from walking up and down on it.'" The Earth and all its fullness is home to Satan. The third planet from the sun is the crown jewel of the universe. Knowing this truth, the devil fights to stay here and rule. To sustain his influence, Satan roams throughout society to lie, deceive, pervert, and murder.

Satan's prideful fall from perfection began before the creation of Adam and Eve. The pericope in Isaiah 14:12–19 gives the effect of the first act of sin in the universe, "How you are fallen from heaven, O Day Star [Lucifer], son of Dawn!" From the Latin, *lucem ferre* translates to mean "light-bearer" or "the morning star, the planet Venus." As indicative in the story of Job, the collapse of Satan from his flawless angelic state did not change the devil's ability to access God's throne. The situation seemingly remains unchanged today.

In the church age, the angelic host will be summoned by God, and Satan can appear in the throne room of the celestial heaven. If questioned about a certain matter, the devil will speak. In Job's case, God's desire was to call the devil's attention to His servant Job and grant certain permissions to test him. When the devil is before the heavenly throne, it gives opportunity to accuse people in service to God.

In the end-times, Satan and all of his associates will be

cast away from the angelic assembly. The primary scriptural evidence for Satan being finally barred from heaven is found in Revelation 12:7–9. The eschatological event inaugurates the kingdom of God and the authority of the Messiah.

> And war broke out in heaven; Michael and his angels fought against the dragon. The dragon and his angels fought back, but they were defeated, and there was no longer any place for them in heaven. The great dragon was thrown down, that ancient serpent, who is called the Devil and Satan, the deceiver of the whole world —he was thrown down to the earth, and his angels were thrown down with him.

Satan and his demonic army take an interest in destroying the overall social order and structure of society. The devil works from a broad base to keep people from salvation and to instigate dissention. Demons can prompt government administrations and provoke heads of state. Leaders of various nations and terrorist-based organizations fall under the devil's persuasion. Full-blown satanic agency arises when wicked individuals mislead nations. The perpetrators of the Holocaust are a prime example. Their actions caused suffering and death to millions of innocent people, disarray to the due order of society, and grievous loss to the world in general.

In order to destroy one's eternal soul, Satan and his fallen angels work through multiple channels. Demonic forces can manifest through self-serving business organizations, the humanism philosophy of educational institutions, or in atheistic movements that take root in society. In Hollywood productions, story lines normally appear that overlook God in human affairs. The implicit intent is to dissuade people from the reality of a higher being and the ultimate truth of salvation through Jesus Christ. As the practice of discounting the gospel continues, people grow distant from the message and can eventually die in their sins. The soul will then depart to the underworld, the material Hades.

The devil provides leadership to the spiritual domain of Hades. He is the operative behind a complex of evil on the earth. A spirit of lawlessness, of darkness, and of rebellion manifests through destructive influence and evil deeds. Satan wields impressive muscle and sway around the globe in his age-long, worldwide effort to bring people and their souls to ruin. Many wicked activities such as human trafficking operate under satanic coercion. Lack of regard for human dignity is the trademark of the devil. Agents of Satan will end up as casualties themselves—perhaps in this life and most certainly in the next. No real victory can be found in allegiance to him.

While discussing Satan's evil empire, it is important to remember that demonic influence is only a small part of the reason why people behave immorally and commit harmful deeds. The act of sinning comes primarily from our own fallen nature, which yields to temptation. Through Adam, the inclination to sin entered the human race, and people became separated from God. In thought and attitude, one can sin minute by minute, hour by hour, and day after day for years at a time and not even be fully aware of the situation. Haughtiness, stinginess, lustful desires, deceitfulness, vengeance, and a host of other ills find acceptance, becoming rooted in our soul.

Scripture presents the idea of Satan being a created angelic being, who clearly lacks the divine attributes of Jehovah. His high rank as an archangel affords him great command and authority, as well as superhuman power and might. Yet unlike God, Satan is not all-powerful (omnipotent), all-knowing (omniscient), or found everywhere (omnipresent). The devil can only be in one place at a time, and his movements find restriction under the divine authority of the Most High. Biblical references such as "ruler of this age," "god of this world," and the "prince of the power of the air" imply space and time limitations.

The story of Job in the Old Testament is an example where

Satan attacks people directly. In the narrative, we see the Lord God lowering the protective hedge around His faithful servant. Job 2:6 tells us, "The Lord said to Satan, 'Very well, he is in your power; only spare his life.'" After taking Job's property and children in an earlier scene, Satan goes on to afflict his body with painful boils and sores from head to toe. Satan is still out to accuse and to do violence to humans throughout the planet. One perceives boundaries being set in place by God, in order to protect humanity from this overpowering foe.

The Bible tells us that Satan is limited, judged, and heading for final sentencing. At the end of the age, this evil being will be sent to a Venus-like planet. The torment of the devil will be "day and night" in the lake of fire (Rev. 20:10). The removal of Satan from the earth completely dethrones him. His reaction is one of personal anguish, resulting from his loss of authority and influence. The judgment of his cadre of demons is likely to occur when the spiritual domain of Hades is thrown into the lake of fire. Matthew 25:41 speaks of the eternal fire being prepared for both Satan and his fallen angels.

One exception to the devil's influence on Earth is during the millennium, when Satan is bound for the entire time. Revelation 20:2–3 tells of an angel who, "seized the dragon, that ancient serpent, who is the Devil and Satan, and bound him for a thousand years, and threw him into the pit, and locked and sealed it over him, so that he would deceive the nations no more, until the thousand years were ended." During the millennium, the influence of Satan on the planet is nonexistent, as the ruler of darkness suffers confinement in the underworld.

In terms of Christian demonology, the Bible considers a demon to be a fallen angel or unclean spirit. Scripture divides these invisible beings into two distinct groups. One set of demons is free and active to roam about on the planet. A second company of demons is in underworld internment, similar to Satan's millennial experience. This simplified figure shows the breakdown:

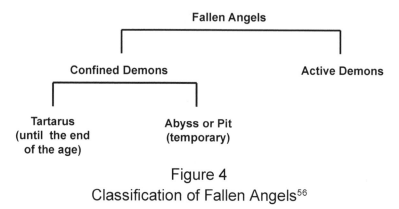

Figure 4
Classification of Fallen Angels[56]

Active demons are present on the planet during the church age and work not only to deceive the mind, but to enter the consciousness of people. In the Gospels, the sinister effect of demonic possession is evident in certain individuals. In Mark 1:21–28, Jesus encounters a man possessed by a demon in a synagogue in Capernaum. In Mark 5:1–20, Jesus and the disciples enter the country of the Gerasenes and come across a man possessed by a legion, or large number of demons. Being intelligent, demons communicate freely through the person. Jesus exercises authority over the evil spirits in order to free the individual from bondage.

Confined demons, being held to the inner darkness of the earth, fall into two categories. One group is in chains until the Day of Judgment at the end of the age. The following scriptures portray the state of those in permanent captivity:

> 2 Peter 2:4—For if God did not spare the angels when they sinned, but cast them into hell [*tartaroo*] and committed them to chains of deepest darkness to be kept until the judgment ...

> Jude 1:6—And the angels who did not keep their own position, but left their proper dwelling, he has

56 Charles C. Ryrie, *A Survey of Bible Doctrine* (Chicago: Moody, 1972), 97.

kept in eternal chains in deepest darkness for the judgment of the great day.

In the first passage, the Greek verb *tartaroo* translates "cast into Tartarus." The term appears once in the Bible and indicates there is a location in the underworld of physical Hades where God imprisons demonic beings who have committed the heinous transgression of abandoning their appropriate living quarters. These spirits will not see the light of day until cast into the lake of fire. The chains indicate evil spirits prefer to be free in order to roam the planet, rather than be held in the netherworld.

A second group of demons is in temporary confinement in the abyss or pit. These evil beings are scheduled for release during the tribulation period. The following scriptural passages support the restrained militia:

> Luke 8:30–31—Jesus then asked him, "What is your name?" He said, "Legion"; for many demons had entered him. They begged him not to order them to go back into the abyss.

> Revelation 9:2–3—He opened the shaft of the bottomless pit, and from the shaft rose smoke like the smoke of a great furnace, and the sun and the air were darkened with the smoke from the shaft. Then from the smoke came locusts on the earth, and they were given authority like the authority of scorpions of the earth.

Without the clear support of the Bible, it would be hard to imagine alien life appearing on the planet in the form of giant mutants. In Revelation 9:2–3, the timetable for release of the second group of confined demons is during the blowing of the fifth trumpet. The leader of the invading army is Abaddon (Heb.) or Apollyon (Gr.), who is the destroyer or angel of the abyss.

Revelation 9:1–11 covers the entire span of events, including a physical description of the beasts. The creatures approach the size of a horse, but a thin exoskeletal structure lightens the body weight. A face and long hair bring anthropomorphic features to the external anatomy. A light-colored circlet appears on the head. It is the "crown of gold" insignia, representing sanction from God. The long, sharp teeth of a lion imply ferociousness. Scales cover large portions of the extremities. An instinctive weapon, a stinging scorpion's tail, extends out the hindquarters. The beasts are alarming to look upon.

Like swarming insects, multitudes of invaders move in hordes to quickly cover the planet. The spreading of the wings can power flight and the bowed legs bring long jump capability to a maneuverable body. The approaching cacophony of shrieks, hopping legs and moving wings brings to mind a pursuing militia riding atop horses and chariots. The reverberation is of galloping hoofs, interspersed by loud screeches of squeaky metal and wood.

Figure 5
The Locust Invasion of Rev. 9:1–11

The invaders are on the offensive and out to molest anyone who does not have the "seal of God" on their forehead, a term not meant to imply a physical mark on the skin, but rather, those who have an unresponsive or inappropriate attitude toward God. The aggressive militia marches to engage in war with the peoples of the earth for five long months—not to kill, but to inflict pain and torture with a stinging tail. Close encounters of the worst kind can only be expected. These creatures are insightful, callous, and persistent.

Intelligence gathering through high-resolution satellite imagery or drone surveillance aircraft may be good for assessing the extent of the invasion but will do little to thwart the systematic advance of these cockroaches. The condition of the nations is dire at the time of the raid, limiting countermeasures. The previous four trumpets (Rev. 8:7–12) describe global catastrophes that have devastating consequences on the population, decisively weakening military resistance. Demons normally attack people at their most vulnerable time, and this incursion is no different. It will be difficult to rally troops or to mount a resistance.

Defense using lethal force is fair game but will have limited effectiveness. The locusts are large targets, but nimble and fast-moving. One can envision the attempted use of handguns, assault rifles, artillery, tanks, and attack helicopters. The state rule remaining after the global upheaval will unite in attempting to eradicate the infestation. A few battles may be won, but the war will be lost. By sheer numbers, the invaders will succeed in accomplishing their primary objective. Targeted individuals stung by the tail will be in relentless pain, wishing for death rather than life. Apparently, modern medicine will not be effective against the venom.

The Soul and Immortal Spiritual Body

The idea of body and soul has biblical roots in the creation story of Genesis. In Genesis 2:7 we read, "Then the Lord God formed man from the dust of the ground, and breathed into his nostrils the breath of life; and the man became a living being." The word "being" (Heb. *nephesh*) can translate as soul, which properly means a "breathing creature" of vitality.

The elements in the dust of the earth are the basic building blocks for the human body. The biological assembly amasses through the molecular rearrangement of elements into compounds. The body of Adam did not contain any life in and of itself. Initially, he was a motionless corpse of flesh and bone. God infused a vibrant soul into the lifeless organism, in order to create a living, breathing being. The soul contains the nonphysical aspects of the person, giving essence and vitality to the physical body.

In the pursuit of addressing the fundamental issues of life, philosophers have systematically engaged in the understanding of one's being. Through rational argument, these thinkers consider the soul to be the incorporeal essence of a person or living thing. Important Greek philosophers such as Socrates and Plato taught about the existence of a soul, which contains the real or transcendent person. Each held to the belief of a soul continuing to live on in a future body. Aristotle thought the soul to be an integral part of the physical body, while considering the human intellect to be never-ending.

The concept of a soul separates in two distinct arenas, centering either on temporal, animate life functions or on spiritual character aiming toward perpetuity. In either perspective, the soul references the mental underpinning and emotional makeup of the person. It contains the seat of the deepest and truest nature, giving personality to the individual.

Natural philosophies give temporal, rather than eternal,

consciousness to the soul. The field of psychology incorporates the ideas of natural philosophy. It is common in the sphere of studying the human mind to reference the soul as the nonphysical, distinct, yet mortal aspect of an individual. The soul is the complex of human attributes, contributing to thoughts, attitudes, behaviors and feelings.

The Bible suggests a partition into three different areas for the individual—the body, the soul, and the spirit. In 1 Thessalonians 5:23, Paul gives a final exhortation to his fellow brothers and sisters, saying, "May the God of peace himself sanctify you entirely; and may your spirit and soul and body be kept sound and blameless at the coming of our Lord Jesus Christ."

The living, breathing human is a unity of body, soul and spirit. When speaking of the body, Scripture considers the person from a temporal standpoint. When speaking of the soul or spirit, the biblical text references the eternal aspects of the individual. The following illustration of concentric circles serves to denote the mortal body in gray and the eternal soul and spirit in white.

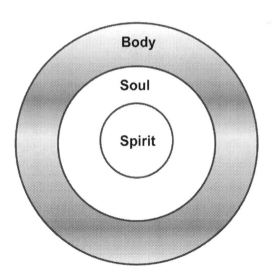

Figure 6
Depiction of Body, Soul and Spirit

The inner circle representing the spirit contains the conscience, which provides for judgment by making rulings toward particular thoughts and behaviors. The conscience governs the individual by performing ethical functions, such as distinguishing right from wrong. The spirit can act in an intuitive role as well, through promptings that help to discern the particular actions of others. The spirit of a person can be indwelled by the Holy Spirit. Paul brings this understanding to bear in Romans 9:1, saying, "I am speaking the truth in Christ—I am not lying; my conscience confirms it by the Holy Spirit."

The middle circle represents the soul, containing the mind, will, and emotions. At death, the soul and spirit depart together in unison. When Jacob's wife, Rachel, died during childbirth, the text states, "As her soul was departing (for she died), she named him Ben-oni, but his father called him Benjamin" (Gen. 35:18). Scripture suggests the material form of the soul mirrors the physical body of the person. Again, in the Old Testament, King Saul goes to the medium of Endor, in order to call up the dead prophet Samuel. In asking the psychic to describe his appearance, she states, "An old man is coming up; he is wrapped in a robe" (1 Sam. 28:14).

The outer circle references the corporal aspects of an individual, which contain the five senses (sight, hearing, smell, touch, and taste) used to contact the material realm. The bulk of the human mass consists of a head, a neck, a torso, two arms with hands, and two legs with feet. Numerous biological systems operate within the body to ensure continual life and health. The composite structure of a human being with its internal organs and external parts will break down and die, returning to dust. A person is dualistic in the sense of having a temporal body but housing an eternal soul and spirit.

In discussing life after death and the eternal realm, the author uses the word "soul" to mean both "soul and spirit." As shown in figure 5, the souls of the righteous and the unrighteous will depart the earthly environment, heading for either the celestial heaven or Hades. These are the two physical locations that accommodate the spiritual essence of the soul. The soul is an intermediate state; that is, it is a temporary mode of existence between physical death and universal resurrection.

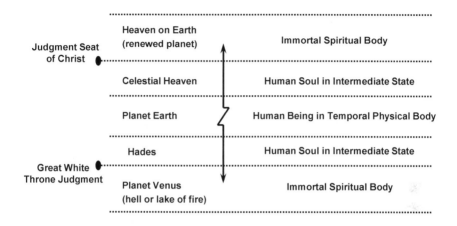

Figure 7
The Dual Paths of the Spiritual World

Following the up arrow, the diagram shows the righteous soul in the intermediate state, residing in the celestial heaven. The term "celestial heaven" substitutes in the text for "third heaven" or paradise. In 2 Corinthians 12:2–4, Paul discusses being caught up in the third heaven and hearing things that no mortal should repeat. Most likely, Paul is describing an experience where he was brought up into the presence of God. He considers the occurrence as extraordinary, but does not use it to boast or exalt himself.

The down arrow has the unrighteous soul going to Hades. The dark netherworld of gloom is a diametrically opposed state of affairs in comparison to the celestial heaven. Hades is a place of separation from God. It is a form of incarceration that lacks in any satisfaction or contentment. Human souls are in a world of colorless suspension, awaiting final sentencing.

The return of Christ to the earth brings an end to the intermediate state. It is a time when every soul receives resurrection and is clothed with an immortal spiritual body. Whether God deems one righteous or unrighteous does not change the fact that every soul becomes an immortal spiritual body. Final resurrection is to life or to condemnation (John 5:29). The righteous will receive rewards at the Judgment Seat of Christ, while the unrighteous face the Great White Throne Judgment.

The immortal spiritual body will be the eternal state for all humanity, the quintessential expression of being, which can function in perfect harmony with the physical environment. The essence is *immortal* in the sense of being able to live in perpetuity. The essence is *spiritual* in the sense of retaining the attributes of the individual's soul and spirit. The essence is a *body* because it has the physical appearance and anatomical members of a human being (1 Cor. 15:42–4).

Following the resurrection, Jesus verifies his physical presence by allowing himself to be touched and by consuming a piece of broiled fish (Luke 24:42–3). These two activities authenticate the bodily resurrection, which is in the form of an immortal spiritual body. Jesus's body is the prototype for every inhabitant of Earth and Venus in the hereafter. For the saved, the furnishing of an immortal spiritual body (following the up arrow) is for a joyous life on Earth. For the unsaved, the furnishing of an immortal spiritual body (following the down arrow) is for a gloomy existence on a planet such as Venus.

The resurrection of Jesus did more than verify His physical presence. On the road to Emmaus, Jesus walks with two disciples for an unspecified distance (Luke 24:13–32). His resurrected body can balance, coordinate, and move forward like a mortal physical body. This act shows the immortal spiritual body has mass and gravitational attraction to the earth.

Walking pushes the body ahead as the leg steps out. The foot contacts the ground and remains stationary until the muscular pull of the leg lifts the back foot and advances it forward. Legs and feet work together in order to propel the individual. The static friction force between the underside of the foot and the ground holds the foot in position. The momentary lock allows the body to overcome air resistance and move forward.

The ability of the resurrected Christ to successfully walk upon the earth demonstrates that the immortal spiritual body is biomechanically created to cooperate with the physics of a planetary environment. The gravitational attraction of the immortal spiritual body to the earth is the key to the entire interaction. The gravitational force on Venus is 90% of the level of Earth, so the inner planet can also facilitate the ability of an immortal spiritual body to move forward. The Venusian surface is under high atmospheric pressure, which works to counter the effects of slightly lower gravitational forces.

The ascension of the Lord is important in a spiritual sense, but it is illuminating from a scientific standpoint as well. At the departure of Jesus from Earth to heaven, as recorded in Acts 1:9–11, His immortal spiritual body, bound to the planet by gravity, is divinely lifted up into the clouds and out of sight of the disciples. In having rest mass, the immortal spiritual body of Jesus requires an external divine force to overcome the attraction to the earth. The "ascension" counters the natural gravitational attraction the physical body and Earth normally exert upon each other.

The Discovery of Soul Substance

The soul is the intermediate state of an individual's afterlife. It is a transitional state between the temporal physical body and the immortal spiritual body, occupying either Hades or the celestial heaven. The soul itself consists of "soul substance." To preserve one's genetic makeup, it is reasonable to believe DNA, the code of life, replicates in soul substance. God may use existing particles in creation to form the constituent building blocks of the soul. Soul substance may be intrinsic in the universe and consist of elementary or fundamental particles such as quarks, leptons, bosons or neutrinos.

With elementary matter built into subatomic or atomic

particles to form structure, the soul will have quantitative physical weight and occupy three-dimensional space. Demonstrating soul substance has mass will not only substantiate the existence of the soul, but draw conclusions for the soul occupying physical space and being subject to gravitational forces.

The journey into the afterlife begins with the soul leaving the body at the point of death. The experimental evidence of soul substance is examined through the early twentieth-century research of Duncan MacDougall, MD, of Haverhill, Massachusetts. MacDougall, who performed his research under closely monitored and controlled conditions, recorded that immediately following death a small loss of body weight was experienced. This minor weight loss is thought to represent the departure of the soul from the physical body. MacDougall's final test report, published in 1907, provides scientific proof that the soul has measureable weight.[57]

The MacDougall report begins by asserting that if the psychic functions of the mind continue after bodily death, then the content of those functions can only exist in a space-occupying body. The space-occupying body must include physical mass and be subject to the laws of gravity. Contained in the body is personal identity; that is, one's personality and consciousness, the essence of which MacDougall considers to be soul substance.[58]

In keeping with universal physical laws, MacDougall refutes the notion of soul substance consisting of nongravitational matter (which he calls ether). Soul substance, he says, has to be organically linked, at least in part, with the human body, which has weight under the force of gravity. If the body is subject to the laws of gravity, so must be the soul as it leaves a deceased body. He concludes in his pretest hypothesis that with proper weighing instrumentation, detection of the soul's departure is possible.

A review of the medical journal article allows one to envision

---

57 Duncan MacDougall, "Hypothesis Concerning Soul Substance Together with Experimental Evidence of the Existence of Such Substance," *American Society for Physical Research*, 1, No. 5 (May 1907): 237–244.
58 Ibid., 237.

MacDougall's test setup and procedure. Placement of dying patients is on an overhead platform containing a bed, pillow, and bed sheets. Below the patient, the sensitive horizontal pendulum of a balancing scale achieves central equilibrium with respect to the overhead staging. The highly responsive "beam and poise" model allows for close visual monitoring of the floating end of the horizontal pendulum, which gives indication of weight loss.

It is important to note the timing for the release of the weighing tool to the marketplace. The scale design became commercially available for sale in 1904 and is still in widespread use today. Similar-type scales find application at the doctor's office or at one's gym or fitness center. In the early twentieth century, the balancing mechanism was cutting-edge technology. Introduced by the Toledo Computing Scale Company, the pendulum-arm scale uses the counterbalance method, where weight compensates for weight. It is a blueprint for accuracy, reliability, and repeatability.[59]

Hard limits to upper and lower travel of the floating end of the balance beam exist at the top and bottom of the slot. With a centered beam, it took 0.2 oz. (5.7 grams) of added weight to drop the beam to the bottom of the slot. Conversely, removing 0.2 oz. (5.7 grams) would lift the beam to the top of the slot. The sensitivity of the scale is fully established in the test setup. If weight changes occur beyond the hard stop of the slot, the equipment is rebalanced to center the pendulum arm.[60]

The experiment begins by placing an individual on the overhead platform and balancing the beam. A synopsis of

---

59 Before 1900, spring tension was the primary method available for weighing objects. The accuracy of a spring tension scale varies with temperature and the springs tend to fatigue over time. These shortcomings made the balance scale far superior. The company slogan for the product was "No Springs, Honest Weight."

60 The necessity to rebalance outside the range of the floating arm introduces some deadband in the test setup. Deadband is the brief interval in the test progression where activity (e.g., increasing or decreasing weight) is not measureable.

the test results for six patients who die naturally during the experiment is presented in table 1 below:

Patient	Final Unaccounted Loss in Weight	Sudden and Ensuing Loss	Notes
1 – Male	0.75 oz. (21.3 g)	0.75 oz. (21.3 g) No ensuing loss	Sudden and distinct drop of 0.75 oz. at death.
2 - Male	1.5 oz. 50 grains (45.8 g)	0.5 oz. (14.2 g) and 1 oz. 50 grains	Sudden drop of 0.5 oz. with later loss of 1 oz. 50 grains.
3 - Male	1.5 oz. (42.5 g)	0.5 oz. (14.2 g) and 1 oz.	Sudden drop of 0.5 oz. with later loss of 1 oz.
4 - Female	No data	No data	Scales not finely adjusted. External interference with test.
5 - Male	0.375 oz. (10.6 g)	0.375 oz. (10.6 g) No ensuing loss	Sudden and distinct drop of 0.375 oz.
6 - Not reported	Test failed	Test failed	Patient died during final scale beam adjustment.

Table 1
Summary of MacDougall's Experimental Results

With respect to the social ethics of the test, I am quite sensitive to the fact that using dying people in an experiment is a rather unsympathetic, even morbid undertaking. One may ask, "Who are these people?" The answer is that we do not know. Should not family, friends, nurses, and doctors be comforting these individuals in their final hour? Well, I think the answer is certainly so! The only detail from the test report is that these individuals bravely volunteered and gave consent to the experiment weeks before death and that the test did not subject the patients to any additional suffering.[61]

The research by MacDougall attempts to follow the scientific method of data acquisition. To be termed scientific, the process of investigation utilizes observable and measurable data, subject to principles of human reason. The primary goal of scientific test methodology is to meticulously accumulate selective information in the form of numerical data. The statistics must not only be accurate, but repeatable. Scientific methodology directs testing be performed under controlled conditions. Being able to reproduce the test configuration in future experimentation using similar equipment is part of the objective.

Discussing the findings requires removing any apprehension or doubt surrounding the validity of the experiment. People can be skeptical of a test conducted in the early 1900s. A research report dating back over one hundred years may seem archaic to some, casting reservation on the conclusions. Some have thought the test set up to be unstable. Others are not completely convinced the weighing system was isolated from perturbations in the human body or from the physical environment. The following discussion will show there is no quantitative basis for rejecting the test results.

A lack of confidence can derive from reading pessimistic articles on collaboratively edited encyclopedia websites such

---

61   Ibid., 238–9.

as Wikipedia. In the biography of Duncan MacDougall (doctor), volunteer contributors add personal comments, claiming the investigative results were "flawed" due to lack of sufficient control over the experimental conditions.[62] The brazen statements are backed up by citing books written by atheists and religious skeptics. Using these resources to draw sharp, negative conclusions about MacDougall's weight measurement experiment is irresponsible and lacks credibility in the best light.

In 2010, the *Journal of Scientific Exploration* published an important research paper, written by Masayoshi Ishida, addressing the various criticisms expressed concerning Dr. Duncan MacDougall's experiment. Ishida uses a technical foundation for understanding MacDougall's test setup, capabilities, and parameters.[63] He successfully addresses the following negative critiques from times past:

1. The experiment was not adequately controlled because of perspiration loss and air currents.
2. The time of death of the patients could not be accurately discerned.
3. The ability to measure weight changes was too imprecise.
4. The cessation of breathing and the heartbeat after death may explain the missing weight.
5. Postmortem body swelling creates a buoyancy force that may explain the missing weight.
6. The small sample size of the experiment makes the results unimportant.

Masayoshi Ishida employs a scientific math modeling technique to analyze the test setup by creating a differential

---

62 Wikipedia, "Duncan MacDougall," http://en.wikipedia.org/wiki/Duncan_MacDougall_(doctor) (accessed July 17, 2014).

63 Masayoshi Ishida, "Rebuttal to Claimed Refutations of Duncan MacDougall's Experiment on Human Weight Change at the Moment of Death," *Journal of Scientific Exploration*, 24, No. 1 (Spring 2010): 5–39.

equation for inputting established constants and variables, in order to assess the true validity of the test. One must put forth "real work" before making either positive or negative statements about the research of another person. The undertaking goes beyond back-of-the-envelope calculations, avoiding oversimplification or hand waving of test concerns. Rather, thoughtful investigation is fundamental to his effort. An evaluator needs to have an honest approach and legitimate interest in examining MacDougall's experiment.

A mathematical representation of the weighing system presents the best problem-solving approach. In order to achieve correspondence to the MacDougall experiment, Ishida makes use of a similar 2001 test setup that attempts to measure the weight change of sheep upon death. The test arrangement is in open air and duplicates the MacDougall experiment, except for the weighing system use of load cells. A load cell is a transducer that converts weight or force into an electrical signal. Load cells are highly sensitive scientific tools of modern weighing technology.[64]

Ishida uses a second order, linear differential equation for a damped vibration model to analyze the weight experiment.[65] Differential equations are a form of calculus; calculus is a mathematical study of change, and differential calculus is the study of the rate of change. In a weight experiment that uses

---

64 Load cells normally consist of a strain gauge placed inside a Wheatstone bridge configuration. A Wheatstone bridge is an electrical circuit that measures changes in electrical resistance. It balances two branches inside a circuit. For weight measurements, one leg contains a strain gauge, acting as a changeable resistive component. The sensor puts out a resistance value both at the "no load" and "load" condition. The difference in value will measure the weight change.

65 The basic differential equation for a damped vibration model under an externally applied force is expressed as $x'' + 2\sigma x' + \omega_n^2 x = F(t)/m$, where x is the small displacement in the system, σ is the vibration decay rate, ω (= $k_{eq}/m)^{0.5}$ is the natural angular frequency of the system, k_{eq} is the equivalent spring constant of the system, $F(t)$ is the time dependent external force applied and m is the total mass of the system. Ishida, "Rebuttal to Claimed Refutations," 10.

living bodies, Ishida must employ calculus to gain a more precise understanding of the nature of motion within the system.

Cardiac and breathing activity creates a vibration disturbance, which could have impacted MacDougall's test. Ishida must determine the response of the weighing system to the disturbance over the time interval of the experiment. Incorporating a level of natural damping or vibration decay within the model is an inherent and necessary part of the assessment.

Understanding how the system reacts to the final disturbance of "cessation of cardiac and breathing" is important for doing error analysis. The boundaries for the system response are between the two farthest points: (a) zero weight loss at death and (b) the maximum 21 grams weight loss at death. Using the 2001 study, Ishida accurately deduces a spring constant, a natural angular frequency, and a vibration decay rate for the MacDougall test setup.

The parametric simulation also employs environmental conditions for an open-air experiment. Ishida must incorporate human body weight, heart rhythm, breathing rate, and weight loss rate due to perspiration. After inputting these baseline parameters, he numerically solves the linear differential equation and determines the system response levels for the duration of the test (a.k.a. noise plots).

Once the assessment is complete for the stated boundary conditions, Ishida is ready to take on MacDougall's critics. The appropriate negation to each criticism previously shown is listed in corresponding numerical order:

1. Ishida assumes a perspiration weight-loss rate of 28.53 grams/hour before death and 14.2 grams/hour after death. The rates have little effect on test sensitivity or conclusions. With the necessary control of bed sheets covering patients in place, the maximum (worst-case) moisture loss during life-to-death transitions does not exceed 2 grams.

Ishida then addresses the concern of convection air currents with calculations showing the effect to be practically nonexistent.

2. Patients 1 and 5 experience sudden death with an abrupt and clearly discernible weight loss. Slower weight loss due to gradual death and ongoing evaporation (patients 2 and 3) identifies as a second mode in the MacDougall report. The exact time of death is less discernible in the second mode, but abnormally high weight loss is evident over the short time of expiration, making the test cases valid.

3. The sensitivity of MacDougall's scale (5.7 grams) is adequate for the test. Using modern load cells would have provided twice the sensitivity. The increased sensitivity and continuous signal output of the transducer could help to detect moisture loss but has no clear benefit in identifying large (10–20 grams) losses in weight seen at death.

4. Noise plots of the system response (the graphs are available in the Ishida report) clearly refute weight loss due to dynamic effects. The high peak-to-peak vibration due to breathing and heartbeat disturbances damp out quickly at death, leaving a stable and clearly discernible system response signature. This is true for both the "no weight loss" and "21-grams weight loss" condition.

5. In order to produce buoyancy that would affect the test, the swelling of the body would have to be unusual or even extraordinary (greater than 14% by volume for a 137-pound subject). Forensics by MacDougall or his colleagues did not report any such occurrence.

6. The four test cases are a small sample size, but they stand as pioneering research because the engineering model cannot logically or analytically dispute the results.[66] The test methodology, measuring techniques

---

66 Ibid., 23.

and observations are seen as valid. Future testing under identical control conditions is likely to produce similar data.

The cessation of all biological functions sustaining an organism brings death. Normally, the life-to-death transition occurs with no change in body weight. Yet, the four cases presented above clearly document large decreases in weight from 10.6 grams to 21.3 grams at the time of death. The only relevant factor to consider is moisture loss from the body. For a two-minute life-to-death transition, this would only account for 1 or 2 grams. Since the large loss of weight is not of natural origin, one must consider MacDougall's detection of soul substance valid. Being subject to gravitational forces, the mass of the departing soul registers as weight loss when using a well-configured and instrumented scale arrangement.

Since the departing soul has evident weight, subject to measurability in a field of gravity, it is safe to construe a direct mortal to immortal transition in our space and time continuum. In having fixed weight, one can infer soul substance has a space occupying volume containing all the mass. It is a reasonable deduction that the continuation of being, or the continuation of conscious ego, would have physical mass, be contained volumetrically, and be detectable when departing a body. We can conclude from the test results that there is credibility to the material departure of the soul from the body at death.

In recalling Genesis 35:18, the departure of Rachel's soul occurs exactly at the point of her death. The Bible clearly supports the soul giving the physical body life and vitality; the soul is the incorporeal and enduring aspects of a person. The removal of the soul from the physical body is a natural consequence of physical death. Soul substance provides the material structure through which human beings perpetuate in the afterlife. It contains the complete inner nature of the person, his or her entire personality, and all that pertains to the individual being.

So why is the soul at its departure not visible to doctors, nurses, hospital aides, or loved ones? In discussing faith and the unseen world around us, Paul tells the reader in 2 Corinthians 4:18 that, "what can be seen is temporary, but what cannot be seen is eternal." An eternal soul may have a measureable amount of material weight, but it does not mandate visible observation.

The human eye cannot see the gases contained in the atmosphere, such as nitrogen, oxygen, argon or carbon dioxide, yet all have weight. The radiation in the electromagnetic spectrum is primarily invisible. Many forms of matter and energy filling our world are not able to be seen.

A final thought has to do with density of the soul in relation to the atmosphere. The density (ρ) of air at sea level, measured at a temperature of 68°F, is 1,204 grams/m^3. The density of a substance calculates by dividing mass over volume. Applying the mass/volume relationship to the intermediate state requires dividing the 21 grams of soul substance by the volume of a human body. The computation will determine the approximate density of the soul.

For calculation purposes, we use the shape of a cylinder to determine the volume of a person. For a cylinder, the volumetric equation is $V = \pi r^2 h$. We can assume an average adult height (h) in the early 1900s of 5 feet and 5 inches (1.65 meters) and three different radii (r) of 4, 5, and 6 inches (0.1016 m, 0.127 m and 0.1524 m). Using the three radii creates a range between the largest and smallest volumes possible for a human size. The 21-gram weight of the soul divides by each of the three calculated volumes of 0.0535 m^3, 0.0836 m^3 and 0.1203 m^3. The division yields the three final densities (ρ) of 392.5 grams/m^3, 251.2 grams/m^3, and 174.4 grams/m^3, respectively.

We can compare the three densities of 392.5 grams/m^3, 251.2 grams/m^3, and 174.4 grams/m^3 to the density of air, which is 1,204 grams/m^3. In dividing each of the three densities by the density of air, we arrive at three percentages. It turns out that for a 21-gram soul, the density ranges fractionally from

33% to 21% to 14% of air density. The percentages give good indication that the soul is buoyant and will float in air.

As a cross-check, it is necessary to employ Archimedes's principle, which states that the buoyancy force is equivalent to the weight of the displaced fluid (air). If the buoyancy force exceeds the weight, the soul will tend to rise. Newton's second law of motion can determine the weight (F) imposed by the earth on a floating object. The formula is $F = m\,a$, where (m) is equal to the mass of a soul, which is 21 grams. The acceleration (a) on the soul is the gravitational pull of the earth ($g = 9.8$ m/s^2). The force F multiplies out to be 205.8 gram-m/s^2, which is conveniently written as 0.206 N (newton).

The buoyancy force B of a soul calculates using $B = \rho_f V_d g$, where ρ_f is the density of the fluid (air), V_d is the volume of the displaced body of air, and g is gravitational acceleration. The density of air ρ_f is 1,204 grams/m^3 and g remains at 9.8 m/s^2. For the 21-gram soul, the three volumes displacing air are 0.0535 m^3, 0.0836 m^3, and 0.1203 m^3. The three buoyancy forces determined through multiplication equal 0.631 N, 0.986 N and 1.421 N, respectively. In each case, the buoyancy force of the air exceeds the 0.206 N downward force of the soul substance, causing lifting forces to be imparted. In order to achieve equilibrium, soul substance would rise to a high altitude.

If we assume an external divine power applies some restraint and control, the free-body motion of a soul departing the corpse will depict as floating through the air. One can now see the physical limitations of a soul in the intermediate state. It cannot function on the earth's surface. The soul cannot maintain contact with the ground, but neither can it escape the gravitational attraction of the earth. In order to move about, it must be guided by an external force. In contrast, the immortal spiritual body of the resurrected Christ was easily able to walk on the road to Emmaus. Immortal spiritual bodies have much higher density and are better able to interact with the natural world.

In the core of the earth where Hades is located, the soul of a person would probably not drift. Within the metallic (iron-nickel) core, low gravitational forces exist. The pressure would have to keep the soul secure on the surface of the surrounding environment. The temperature of the inner core is thought to be very high, as much as 9,800°F. The pressure approximation for the Earth's inner core is high as well, ranging from about 3.3 to 3.6 million atmospheres.

No empirical data is available to verify the temperature and pressure in the center of the earth. The environment would certainly be unbearable for any form of life. For afterlife in the intermediate state, the soul would need to tolerate extreme conditions. The density of soul substance is exceedingly low, but the exact elemental makeup is unknown. Since soul substance is composed of unspecified combinations of elementary particles, the survivability cannot be assessed in a scientific manner. Habitation in abysses within the inner core of the earth remains possible for the soul.

Confinement of Souls in Hades

Sheol/Hades remains to this day an underworld place of incarceration. As noted earlier, the Sheol in the Old Testament has become the netherworld of Hades in the New Testament. The primary difference today is the absence of souls from Abraham's bosom, which departed with Jesus for the celestial heaven. The story of the rich man and Lazarus gives clear indication of confinement in Hades for the guilty.

Geologists study the composition and structure of the entire sphere of the earth, which has a diameter of 7,918 miles. In peeling back the globe like an onion, one discovers concentric layering. The planetary shell consists of an outer layer called the crust. The crust encases the planet both continentally and oceanically. The crust extends up to 25 miles below Earth's surface. Sitting below the crust is the predominately solid, two-part mantle layer. The consistency of the mantle is primarily of highly viscous or gummy rock.

The mantle extends for 1,800 miles beneath the crust. Under the mantle and extending for 1,400 miles is the environmentally important liquid outer core, which is composed of molten iron and nickel. Convection currents in the outer core transfer cooler metal down and warmer metal up. The formation of life on Earth may not have been possible without this liquid outer core.[67] Beneath the molten outer core, lies the inner core. The inner core is a firm ball of iron-nickel alloy, continuing for 760 miles to the center of the earth.

The most feasible spot for Sheol/Hades within the geological strata is a void or cavity in the iron-nickel core. Many passages in the Old Testament place an emphasis on the downward direction and extraordinary depth of Sheol. In being made of firm material and situated in the heart of the earth, only the inner core satisfies both the biblical and physical requirements for captivity of soul substance. The molten outer core is flowing and cannot facilitate confinement. Any place in the mantle is not directly below all surface locations and would be offset from the center of the earth.

The physical location of Hades could situate within one or several cavities contained in the volume of the inner core. The radius of the metallic core places the core surface at 3,200 miles below sea level. The radius to the center of the earth is 3,959 miles. Hades can situate at a depth of between 3,200 and 3,959 miles. Interesting support for the earth's core containing lost souls is in the experiential account of Bill Weiss.

---

67 The flow of liquid metal in the outer core generates electric currents, which in turn produce the Earth's magnetic field. The magnetic field extends outward from the Earth for several thousand miles to create the magnetosphere, which deflects the solar wind of the sun. Without this field, charged particles would directly strike the Earth's upper atmosphere, stripping away the ozone layer that protects the planet from harmful ultraviolet radiation.

In his book, *23 Minutes in Hell*, he reports the location of Hades to be 3,700 miles below the surface of the planet.[68]

In geophysics, the scientific study of Earth's physical processes requires the use of oceanography, seismology, volcanism, and geomagnetism. Seismological research analyzes the propagation of waves generating from earthquakes and other large-scale seismic sources, such as volcanic eruptions and atomic explosions. Seismic events will generate two primary signal types, known as S-waves and P-waves. Traveling as "body waves" into the interior of the planet, S-wave and P-wave analysis is the primary method for researching the structure of the inner Earth.

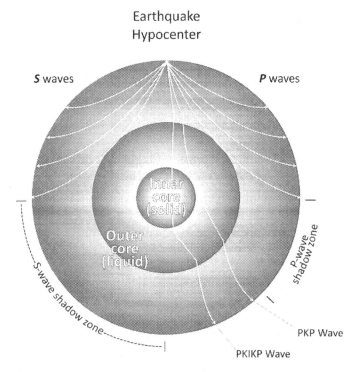

Figure 8
S and P Wave Propagation through the Earth

---

68   Bill Wiese, *23 Minutes in Hell* (Lake Mary, FL: Charisma House, 2006), 107.

Figure 8 depicts an earthquake originating at the hypocenter, the direct site of the tectonic movement. A hypocenter is the focal point of a seismic event where primary and secondary waves begin. The epicenter sits on the earth's surface directly above the hypocenter. The ray diagram shows a representative dispersion of waves passing through the body of the earth.[69]

Primary waves (P-waves) are compression waves; the wave motion and wave propagation are in the same direction. P-waves can readily travel through the earth's continuum, but pathways through the outer or inner core suffer slowing, refraction, and slight attenuation. Secondary waves (S-waves) are shear waves; the wave motion is perpendicular to wave propagation. An S-wave can traverse well in solid material but dwindles rapidly through the viscous liquid of the outer core.

The classification ascribed to the P-wave passing though the outer core is PKP. This wave travels through the mantle (P), crosses into the outer core (K) and returns back out through mantle (P). A P-wave passing through the inner core denotes as PKIKP. This wave travels through the mantle (P), crosses into the outer core (K), and moves into the inner core (I). When the ray departs the inner core, it follows a similar pattern in reverse (KP) to exit the earth and find detection at a seismic station.

Seismologists cannot use PKIKP wave to analyze the solidity of the spherical iron center. Rather, PKIKP waves reveal the material characteristics of the inner core, which have proven to be anisotropic. Anisotropy means the physical properties vary along different directions or axes. For instance, seismic waves traveling from pole to pole through the inner core arrive six seconds faster than seismic waves traveling the same distance on the equatorial plane. The speed of wave travel is

69 The S-wave shadow zone and the P-wave shadow zone locate on both sides of the lower sphere of the earth but are shown separately for clarity. Encyclopedia Britannica, "Primary Wave," http://www.britannica.com/EBchecked/topic/476245/ primary-wave (accessed August 1, 2014).

significantly different along the two major axes, indicating the anisotropic nature of the nickel-iron alloy.[70]

In order to investigate the structural solidity of the inner core and either confirm or deny the presence of voids, seismologists attempt to detect PKJKP waves, rather than PKIKP waves. The PKJKP wave is a shear wave thought to be locally present in the inner core during a seismic event. The letter "J" denotes not just the S-wave, but includes the unique inner core path of the S-wave. Using high quality broadband test arrays, researchers occasionally publish reports analyzing PKJKP waveforms. The technical memorandum will often note the difficulty of the observation.[71]

Data acquisition of PKJKP seismic waves remains elusive and casts doubt on the technical ability to comprehensively evaluate the solidity of the inner core. In 2011, the Scripps Institute of Oceanography issued a report reviewing the stacks of over 90,000 long-period seismograms. The results were not encouraging for detecting S-waves in the inner core. The publication concludes routine observation of the PKJKP phase to be unlikely.[72]

Geophysicists and seismologists face significant challenges assessing the presence or absence of empty spaces in the inner

---

70 The reason for the anisotropy may be due to a uniform orientation of iron crystals in the inner core. The mechanism causing the preferred positioning remains a mystery. Xiaodong Song, "Anisotropy of the Earth's Inner Core," *Reviews of Geophysics,* American Geophysical Union 35, No. 3 (August 1997), 297–313.

71 Support for the PKJKP observation is based on the formulation of a specific set of seismic circumstances and the use of highly sensitive test equipment. A. Cao and B. Romanowicz, "Constraints on Shear Wave Attenuation in the Earth's Inner Core from an Observation of PKJKP," *Geophysical Reserch Letters,* 36, No. 9 (May 2009): 5.

72 The findings of the seismogram search indicate the amplitudes of the PKJKP phase to be significantly smaller than signal-generated noise caused by surface P-waves and reverberations from upper mantle discontinuities. Peter M Shearer, Catherine A Rycher, and Qinya Liu, "On the Visibility of the Inner-core Shear Wave Phase PKJKP at Long Periods," *Geophysics Journal International,* 185, No. 3 (2011): 1379–83.

core, due to the scarcity of PKJKP waves. From a technical perspective, this presents an inability to verify the solidity of the inner core. A solid inner core would cast doubt on Hades being in the center of the earth. Voids in the inner core would leave the door open for spiritual habitation zones. As it is, science may never come to fully understand the detailed structure of the central sphere, making it impossible to either substantiate or to discredit habitation zones for the souls in Hades.

The previous section of this chapter concludes soul substance is subject to the law of gravity, due to a small amount of physical mass. It also occupies a spatial volume that is buoyant in air. Considering these facts, transporting a person's soul to Hades requires a passageway. A natural underground tunnel would begin in the continental crust and extend to the iron core of the earth. An opening on the surface of the earth into the deep mantle has never been found by geologists. However, the lack of such a discovery to date should not be cause to discount the likelihood of its existence.

From a geotechnical engineering perspective, the physical construction of a tunnel into the center of the earth is not possible. Current technology cannot even penetrate the crust of the planet. In 1970, the Soviet Union attempted to drill a hole into the earth at the Kola Peninsula near Finland. Twenty-two years later and 7.6 miles down, the project ended because of the high heat encountered by the drill bit and the stickiness of the rock.

In attempting to find corroboration for an underground corridor, we again touch upon the experiential account of Bill Weiss, who reports traveling through a 35-foot diameter tunnel.[73] The underworld channel would have to been created by divine agency. Confined demons from the locust invasion arise from a passageway described as the "bottomless pit."

---

73 Wiese, *23 Minutes in Hell*, 30.

The mentioning of a bottomless pit is found in other verses of Revelation as well.[74]

One concept of a physical channel would fit well with a bottomless pit. It is a radial tunnel, extending like a spoke from the wheel of a bicycle down to the hub. It would provide the shortest path to Hades. An animal or human being falling into such an opening would experience an almost endless drop, simulating a bottomless pit. A person would reach terminal velocity and travel for over 30 hours before reaching the center of the earth.[75] For the departing soul, a radial tunnel works well. Floating soul substance can be guided down to Hades by an external divine force after leaving the corporeal state.

Arriving in Hades, an impenitent person would quickly learn that the grace and goodness of God is not present. Detention in the inner parts of the planet would lack any pleasure. The chamber would be completely dark and exist under high temperature and pressure. Removing God from any habitation creates a bad situation. The confines are empty of His influence and attributes. The only thing remaining would be despair, torment, misery, and dread. How can there be love or affection, tranquility or rest, joy or contentment without God? In a real sense, Hades is a hot, dim, isolated, and unpleasant holding tank for unrighteous souls waiting for final judgment.

The idea of spiritual contact between demonic beings and human souls in Hades is not supportable in Scripture. Like Satan, demons have to be confined in order to stay in the underworld. The detention of evil spirits in the abode of Tartarus

---

74 Six verses revealing the bottomless pit to be a channel are found in Rev. 9:1, 2, 11; 11:7; 17:8; and 20:1. The beast and other demonic hosts arise from the bottomless pit of the underworld. Coogan, *New Oxford Annotated Bible*, 432–3, 434, 442, 445 [New Testament].

75 In fluid dynamics, terminal velocity is the final speed reached by an object moving through fluid (air) under the force of gravity. Assuming for calculation purposes an unchanging gravitational force and uniform density of air, the speed of a skydiver (122 miles/hr) would have to be maintained for 32.4 hours, in order to reach the center of the earth (3,959 miles).

may indicate an isolated space. The same can be said for the abyss (or pit), where Satan and other demons are kept back for a time. The metallic inner core of the planet is large enough to contain numerous cavities that can be used to house human souls and demons separately.

The temporary confinement of Satan tells of his dislike for the netherworld. The devil has a pervasive desire to be nomadic and roam the surface of the earth, in order to deceive humankind and to practice evil. He wants little to do with the physical location of Hades, though he has aided many in going there. Hollywood sometimes depicts the devil in human form wearing a tight red outfit. He has two horns, an arrowed tail, and brandishes a pitchfork while sitting on his throne. Fire blows from his fingertips as he points in defiance. He seems to enjoy his residence in the inner earth, as he masterminds mayhem. In truth, credence cannot be given to Satan making Hades his home, or in finding any pleasure in an underground abode.

The parable of the rich man and Lazarus depicts a representative scene, where conversation takes place between departed souls. Does conversation continue today? Are those in the underworld sitting in solitary confinement, or do souls situate in a communal jail block? Scripture does not enlighten us on the exact condition in Hades. One could speculate camaraderie would continue to exist following the departure of those in Abraham's bosom.

During incarceration in the underworld, one could plausibly deduce solitary confinement as a method through which some individual receives greater condemnation (Matt. 23:14). The concept is not any different than what exists in a state penitentiary or detention center. The most evil or disruptive individuals receive separate quarters as a penalty for bad behavior. In a dark underworld prison, it would not be out of place for some souls to suffer in isolation.

Is it possible to step back and derive any good news about

Hades? Not really. The residents are simply waiting for the Day of Judgment. Every human being in the netherworld, both small and great, will stand before the throne of God. The souls emptying out of Hades will be equipped with immortal spiritual bodies for a final appearance on the earth's surface. Every person will stand on his or her own accord before the throne. Life reviews will contain acts of sin and individuals will be culpable. Excuses are not acceptable and no advocacy will be available. A finding of guilty is the likely verdict in this court setting.

Transport to the lake of fire is the next phase of perdition. Seeing the renewed planet Earth when departing from the great white throne will not be easy. Lost people have forfeited the privilege of an earthly abode and will be heading to the surface of a dismal planet. Feelings of loss and sorrow will come to those being permanently barred from a beautiful paradise. What follows is the boredom of living on a hot, dry, desolate, and extremely undesirable planet filled with volcanic spew. Being above ground, planets such as Venus are an improved venue over Hades. Nevertheless, they provide little satisfaction for the long term.

CHAPTER 5

Unveiling Venus as Perdition

An intelligent mind acquires knowledge,
and the ear of the wise seeks knowledge.

Proverbs 18:15

By its very nature, the field of planetary science is broad in scope. Studying the evolutionary, physical and orbital characteristics of an entire world is a multidisciplinary task. Performing an assessment of past and present conditions utilizes fields such as astronomy, geology, atmospheric science, chemistry, and space physics. In serving to present an overview of our neighboring planet Venus, this chapter will draw upon these various disciplines.

Comprehensive information pertaining to Venus unfolds slowly over human history. Our review begins with stargazing thousands of years ago by ancient civilizations and ends with present spacecraft exploration by various nations. Outside of the sun and the moon, the planet Venus is the brightest object in the sky, having the unique ability to cast shadows from its position above the horizon. In outshining all other stars and planets, Venus has attracted great attention over the centuries.

The chapter will reveal much about what has been called our "sister" or "twin" planet. The term's use is tongue-in-cheek. The only resemblance between Earth and Venus is in physical size and close orbital proximity. The similarity between terrestrial worlds diminishes greatly upon close examination. The reader will discover that scientific knowledge about the second planet from the sun has grown exponentially since the early 1960s. Up until that time, the planet was shrouded in clouds and able to veil many secrets.

As spacecraft from Earth unmask Venus using scientific instruments, biblical comparisons to the future abode of the unrighteous becomes evident. Radiometers, magnetometers, spectrometers, photopolarimeter imaging systems, synthetic aperture radar (SAR), and surface photography, along with other experiments, assist in bringing new clarity and insight. The chapter relates space mission findings to scriptural references of hell and the lake of fire, culminating in a summary at the end. The recap brings focus to the reality of perdition in our solar system and raises new urgency in avoiding a permanent sentence to any similar place in the cosmos.

Venus through the Naked Eye

The word planet comes from the Greek word *planetes*, meaning wanderer. Without a doubt, Venus is a wanderer in the night sky, being seen both as the "morning star" and the "evening star." Being closer to the sun than Earth, the inner planets of Mercury and Venus can only be seen in close proximity to the sun. The planetary alignment creates viewing times following sunset or before sunrise. As the evening star, Venus drops slowly into the horizon, following the sun after sundown. As the morning star, it rises up from the horizon, leading the sun in the final hours before daybreak.

In the mythology of the ancient Greeks, the captivating glow of the planet was impetus enough to name the celestial body

Aphrodite, the goddess of love. As the daughter of Zeus, she beguiles gods and men alike, laughing sweetly or mockingly at those conquered by her charm and deceit. Adopting the Greek gods, the Romans called her Venus, the goddess of love and beauty. Venus is the only planet named after a female, probably due to the attractiveness of the object in the sky.

The early Egyptian and Chinese cultures mistakenly understood the morning star and evening star as being two different objects in the night sky. Astronomical observations and recordings by the Babylonians confirmed their understanding of Venus as a single celestial body. The clay tablets of Ammisaduqa, compiled in the mid-seventeenth century BC, record Venus setting in the evening, and, at later times, rising in the morning.

In the Americas, the Mayan, Aztec, and Inca civilizations paid close attention to Venus. The Mayans were dedicated astronomers, who mapped out phases of the moon and constructed astronomically aligned shrines. The Mayan structure El Caracol in Chichen Itza, Mexico, is a domed building resembling an observatory. Slots cut out in the rock of the dome look out to points on the celestial sphere, where Mayan astronomer-priests observed heavenly bodies like Venus. The role of the planets in the culture went beyond casual observation, to being objects of worship and markers of times and seasons.

The figure 9 graphic looks down at the sun from above the North Pole, showing Earth and Venus in their respective orbital paths. Venus is at an average distance of 67 million miles from the sun, while the Earth is 93 million miles. Venus not only has a smaller orbital path than the Earth, but because of a stronger gravitational lock to the sun, moves more rapidly in its orbit. Venus regularly passes our world on the inside fast track. The planet manages to complete a single orbit around the sun in only 225 Earth days. On successive views as an evening star, we watch her sprinting to catch up with us. Later, when she appears as a morning star, we are watching her moving away, leaving us trailing behind.

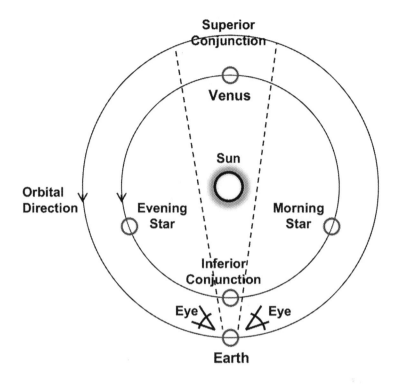

Figure 9
The Viewing of Venus from Earth

Inferior conjunction notes the point where Venus is closest to Earth and superior junction is its furthest distance. The planet is out of view at inferior and superior conjunction. A conjunction occurs when two astronomical objects, such as the sun and Venus, are in close proximity to each other in the sky. The out-of-view window is much greater at superior conjunction than at inferior conjunction.

Earth and Venus, together with the rest of the planets in the solar system, orbit the sun in the counterclockwise direction. Therefore, it takes 584 days of travel for Venus to circle and catch up with the Earth. The two dotted lines in figure 9 cutting through the orbit of Venus divide up the 584-day cycle. The left-side, in-view period for observing the planet is as an evening star in the west. The right-side, in-view period is as a morning star in the east. The out-of-view times, the inferior and superior conjunctions, total about 104 days. This ideally leaves about an eight month window for observing Venus both in the east and west.[76] Geographic location on the earth and occlusion caused by the sun and horizon contribute to reductions in viewing times.

When the Lord God and His people return to Earth, the planet Venus will still be observable in the same manner. The evening star will set in the west and the morning star will rise in the east. The question becomes whether the biblical scriptures authenticate the idea of the righteous in heaven witnessing the fate of the unrighteous in perdition. Intuitively, the idea of heaven as a perfect place of happiness and contentment would tend not to support such a notion.

Support for the freedom to observe the abode of the unrighteous comes from Revelation 14:10, which reads, "they will also drink the wine of God's wrath, poured unmixed into the cup of his anger, and they will be tormented with fire and sulfur in the presence of the holy angels and in the presence of the Lamb."[77] The prophecy condemns the sinful and then announces the viewing of their fate by holy beings. The word for presence (Gr. *enopion*) can mean "in the sight of." Those living in the presence of Jesus Christ will witness the retribution of fire and sulfur toward the guilty.

---

76 Over an eight-year cycle, the planet charts five different patterns in the sky. The variation in the five figures and the observer's latitude can change the in-view times. At its peak, the planet can reach an elevation of 47° above the horizon. Known as maximum elongation, it is the furthest distance Venus can get from the sun. David H. Grinspoon, *Venus Revealed: A New Look Below the Clouds of Our Mysterious Twin Planet* (Reading, MA: Addison-Wesley, 1997), 9–15.

77 John the Baptist bestows the title "Lamb of God" on Jesus in John 1:29. The imagery of the Lamb is drawn from the Passover lamb in Exodus Chpt. 12. Jesus was the sacrificial lamb led to slaughter at His crucifixion. Coogan, *New Oxford Annotated Bible*, 149 [New Testament].

The passage from Isaiah 66:22–24, first reviewed in *Foretelling of the Prophets* (chapter 2), addresses the concept of God's people being able to go out from new moon to new moon to worship the Lord and to "look at the dead bodies of the people who have rebelled against me [God]." The new moon is indicative of God's people living in heaven on Earth; the suffering of the dead includes a worm never dying and an unquenchable fire. In the Hebrew calendar, the new moon marks a time of sanctity and celebration. New moon, or no moon, nights are typically the best time to observe celestial objects such as Venus.

According to Revelation 14:10 and Isaiah 66:22–24, righteous people will be able to witness the fate of the unrighteous. Accomplishing this comes by observing Venus or another celestial body. Finally, from the parable of the rich man and Lazarus (Luke 16), we sense that both Abraham and Lazarus are able to see the sufferings of the rich man firsthand. Situated in Abraham's bosom, the righteous can observe the distress of the unrighteous in an adjacent habitation. Though taking place in Hades before the final judgment, the scene can be understood as foreshadowing a time when God's people on Earth will look upon the dismal abode of Venus.

Venus through the Telescope

Using a telescope, one would think astronomers could gain significant knowledge about Venus. After all, magnification of Mars could distinguish the polar ice caps and help determine the planet's rotation period and axial tilt. In the Jovian system, consisting of Jupiter and its moons, the use of optics could document the Great Red Spot and identify several moons. Pointed toward Saturn, the telescope was able to see natural satellites and the amazing rings around the planet.

Our neighboring inner planet, however, is not amicable to visual observation. The perfect defense against optical instruments is perpetual, featureless cloud cover. Seen through the telescope, the surface of Venus presents a yellow-white tinge of color, but is otherwise completely bare and lacking detail. Unbeknownst to the early observers, the yellow-white coloration can hint of sulfuric acid, a clear-yellow chemical in the cloud cover.

The initial observation of Venus through a telescope was in 1610 by Galileo Galilei, the Italian astronomer and mathematician. Optical tools facilitate viewing Venus as a disc, rather than the pinpoint of a star. Being the first to analyze the planet in this manner, Galileo made significant discoveries. First, the disc appears in various phases, like the waxing and waning moon. From the observation, he drew the astronomical conclusion that Venus must orbit the sun. Secondly, the physical size of the phases appears to vary. The following graphic depicts the orbital phases of Venus, which manifest according to the relative position between Venus and Earth.

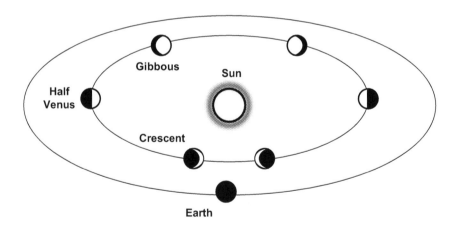

Figure 10
The Orbital Phases of Venus

A full Venus is never observable from Earth because of the sun's occlusion at superior conjunction. A new Venus can only be seen during a transit event, such as that of June 2012. As the evening star, the first sighting of Venus is in the gibbous phase, when the planet is furthest from Earth and displays the smallest angular diameter.[78] The planet moves to become a half Venus before finishing as a crescent. The crescent phase of Venus is closest to Earth and shows the largest size. As the morning star, the planet begins as a crescent and shifts to a half Venus before finishing in the gibbous phase.

Stars and the planets in the solar system are observable on the celestial sphere, the global sky dome surrounding the earth. Astronomers normally measure the angular diameter of celestial objects in degrees that are broken down into arc seconds. An arc second is a unit of angular measurement equal to 1/3600th of one degree. Planets in the solar system and stars range from .005 to 66.0 arc seconds. For the planet Venus, the gibbous phase is around 9.5 arc seconds, and the crescent phase spans 66 arc seconds. The crescent is the largest object in the sky, excluding the sun and the moon.

At inferior conjunction, Venus can pass directly between the Sun and Earth, creating a transit event. As the book cover depicts, Venus is a small dark disk moving across a fiery solar surface. As noted earlier, transits of Venus are rare astronomical occurrences. Even though inferior conjunction occurs every 584 days, the orbital plane of Venus is not directly aligned with Earth. The plane tilts or inclines 3.4° relative to our own, letting Venus pass above or below the sun during most inferior conjunctions.

Transits of Venus take place in pairs, separated by eight years, after which no transit occurs for over a century. There were transit pairs in the years 1631 and 1639, 1761 and 1769, 1874 and 1882, and then 2004 and 2012. Expected future transits are in 2117 and 2125, and in 2247 and 2255.

In 1639, Jeremiah Horrocks and William Crabtree of England

---

78 In astronomy, the sizes of objects in the sky are often given in terms of angular diameter, which is the measured diameter of the object on a flat plane.

became the first people to observe and make record of a transit of Venus. Horrocks used a Galilean type refracting telescope to project the sun's image onto a screen fixed behind the eyepiece. He recorded an apparent diameter of 65 arcseconds.[79] The subsequent transit in 1761 facilitated the discovery of the Venusian cloud cover. Russian scientist Mikhail Lomonosov discerned the planet to have a fuzzy perimeter during the transit and a slight halo at solar ingress and egress. These findings give evidence of a prominent atmosphere surrounding the planet.

The Italian astronomer and Catholic priest of the Jesuit order Giovanni Battista Riccioli was the first to notice a subtle glow emanating from the dark side of Venus. Since his first sighting, many amateur and professional astronomers have observed the phenomenon. Documented in 1643, the event became known as "ashen light." Through the telescope, this radiance appears as a low-level, transient shine or luminosity. Ashen light remains a mystery, although a possible cause is lightning. Concurrent flashes of lightning in the planet's atmosphere over a short interval might give off a glow.

From 1761 until the early 1960s, the power of hope and imagination replaced verifiable facts about Venus. During the two-hundred-year period, wherein major scientific and industrial advancements were made, little knowledge was gained about the inner planet. Specialized machinery came to replace hand production in the factory. Electricity and light bulbs replaced candle light in the home. Modernization brought forth the automobile, the airplane and the mainframe computer. The world moved forward technologically, but the blurry disc of Venus remained a mystery. Many records of telescopic observations are on file with carefully drawn surface features such as continents, polar ice caps, and canals, which amount to little more than inspired fantasy.

---

79 Patrick Moore, *Venus* (Great Britain: Octopus Publishing, 2002), 94.

The thick layer of clouds surrounding Venus led to speculation about a world filled with water. After all, Venus is a terrestrial planet, about the same size as Earth and in the same orbital proximity; perhaps the cloud cover compensates for Venus being closer to the sun and helps retain necessary moisture. Lying beneath the canopy must be a high-humidity planet, experiencing constant rainfall. The steady rain must create marshlands, lakes, rivers, and perhaps even large oceans.

Emerging from the mind's eye was a world filled with jungles and lush tropical rainforests, teeming with dense, impenetrable vegetation and succulent plants. A globe where water and plants exist must support basic biological life or even animal life. So naturally, fish, birds, amphibians, reptiles, and perhaps even mammals could exist on the surface.

In 1918, a book authored by Nobel laureate Svante Arrhenius gave a dramatic and alluring view of the planet Venus. Arrhenius, a Swedish physicist and chemist, received the 1903 Nobel Prize in Chemistry for his discovery of electrolytic dissociation. He later became interested in planetary atmospheres and their role in climate control.

His writing describes Venus as an extremely humid planet covered with swamplands, where everything is dripping wet. He envisions expanses of lush vegetation that are accelerated in growth by dampness and an average temperature of 115°F. Arrhenius compares the planet's evolutionary phase to the Carboniferous Period of Earth, an era of geologic time 360 to 290 million years ago when the vast amount of water and plant life on Earth led to the creation of coal-forming sediments.

Science fiction was one genre used to maintain interest in a vibrant picture of Venus. Academia classifies the late 1930s through 1950s as the Golden Age of Science Fiction writing.[80] Authors such as John W. Campbell, who helped to shape the

---

80 University of Hamburg English Department, "A Virtual Introduction to Science Fiction: Online Toolkit for Teaching SF," http://virtual-sf.com/ (accessed June 4, 2013).

science fiction age, republished *The Black Star Passes* (1953), an account of Venus as the home of an advanced civilization that had to contend with enormous invading aircraft. In the second book of *The Space Trilogy* (1943) titled *Perelandra*, C. S. Lewis describes Venus as an oceanic paradise where remarkable animals live on free-floating rafts of vegetation. In Ray Bradbury's short story collection, *A Medicine for Melancholy* (1959), one finds the provocative narrative, "All Summer in a Day," where a colony living on rainy Venus sees the sun for only one hour every seven years.

Reflecting belief in Venus as a nurturing and populated planet was film and television. The traditional Hollywood gender assigned to the Venusian is female, as the planet's feminine name seemed to dictate the sex of the inhabitants. Law enforcement adventures by *Space Patrol*, an admired 1950s television and radio science fiction series, had an Earth-based interplanetary police force frequently encountering alien outlaws. On swampy, cloud-covered Venus, the crew of patrolling astronauts found a world teeming with dinosaurs and Amazon women. In the popular 1958 film *Queen of Outer Space*, starring Zsa Zsa Gabor, Eric Fleming, and Laurie Mitchell, an all-male crew from Earth crash lands on Venus and discovers a planet filled with eye-catching females. Their incarceration is short-lived, as the women long for the love of men again.

In the 1930s, the surveillance of space began outside the visible spectrum. Astronomers began using radio telescopes (large dish antennas) to look at celestial objects. Radio waves have low electromagnetic opacity, meaning that signal-generating sources travel well through the Earth's atmosphere into space. By the mid-1950s, passive radio observations were giving account of large amounts of microwave radiation being emitted by Venus.

Reports of this finding began to circulate in the scientific community, raising concerns about a hot inner planet. It became necessary to determine the exact location of the radiation, which could either be from the cloud cover or the surface of the planet. The vision of a tropical, moist Venus, teeming with vegetation and animal life, was a bubble on the verge of bursting.

The discovery is a stark reminder of the paradox of the night sky. The luster of the Milky Way, the dazzle of Venus, and the romantic allure of a full moon attach to our emotions. Our home planet is a warm, safe, and beautiful place in the universe. But the reality outside the confines of Earth is the unpleasant, threatening, and inhospitable abode of outer space.

Consider an interesting correlation in the biblical scriptures. In Matthew 8:12, 22:13, and 25:30, Jesus warns people about not being "thrown into the outer darkness, where there will be weeping and gnashing of teeth." Outer darkness is a descriptor of perdition. In the parable in Matthew 22:13, a certain man ends up in outer darkness for not being properly attired for a wedding reception. The wedding celebration is akin to the kingdom of heaven. Bible commentators explain the banquet hall is well lit, so exclusion from the festivity represents outside darkness. Since the other two scriptures make no mention of an indoor social gathering, the rationalization lacks in completeness.

A more fitting explanation is to consider "thrown into the outer darkness" to mean the darkness of the night sky; that is, the blackness of the celestial realm. In the first century travels of Jesus and the apostles, the night firmament was exceedingly dark, the stars filling the visible sky due to the lack of outdoor lights. The Lord is warning against an unrighteous person being thrown (lifted and transported) into the darkness of outer space. The outer darkness of the atmospheric envelope fits with all three warnings made in the scriptures and brings uneasiness not only about the journey, but the final destination.

On a sunny day, the sky of Earth is bright blue because light from the sun scatters and reflects off gas molecules and particulate matter in the air. The atmosphere is brightly lit by sunlight. Beyond our planet, outer space is characteristically black because of the absence of any atmosphere. Sunlight cannot be absorbed or reflected in the vacuum of outer space, so the surroundings lack color or illumination. A voyage exiting Earth on the way to Venus will be shadowy and dark.

In the early 1960s, another technology, radar astronomy, made ground-based contribution to the study of Venus. Radar astronomy bounces radar pulses off nearby objects and analyzes the returning resonance. Following World War II, radar waves echoing off the moon could measure surface roughness. When directed at Venus in 1962, measurements of radar waves uncovered information about axial rotation.

The first detail of the discovery was the directional rotation of Venus, which is backward or retrograde. In relation to the sun and the Earth, the planet spins on its axis in the opposite direction. A person standing on the surface of Venus would see daylight first on the western horizon.

The second point was finding the rotation rate of Venus to be amazingly sluggish, having a sidereal day lasting 243 Earth days. A sidereal day measures one complete spin of a planet relative to a fixed inertial reference frame, such as distant stars. On Earth, a sidereal day last 23 hours, 56 minutes and 4 seconds, while a solar day lasts 24 hours.[81]

So how long does a solar day last on Venus? A solar day measures the apparent time taken for the sun to travel once around the sky and return to the original position, providing one complete "day and night" period to an observer on the planet. A solar day on Venus requires a special computation, which considers the retrograde spin direction, the sidereal day (243 Earth days), and the orbital period around the sun (225 Earth

---

81 The daily difference of 3 minutes and 56 seconds between sidereal and solar time necessitates creating a leap year. The leap year adds the 29th day to the month of February every four years. The additional day keeps the Gregorian calendar year synchronized with the solar year.

days).[82] The calculated time for the event equates to about 117 Earth days.

Knowing a solar day lasts 117 Earth days brings up an interesting observation. The extended time of the Venusian day divides evenly between the daytime and nighttime. From the perspective of a person from Earth, living on the planet Venus would mean having 58½ days of overcast skies between sunrise and sunset, followed by 58½ days of darkness between sunset and sunrise. From an earthly standpoint, the lengths of the day and night are excessive amounts of time.

An expansive understanding of Jesus's warning about being "thrown into the outer darkness" can include not only the journey but the final destination of Venus. People are normally used to about 12 hours of daylight, followed by 12 hours of darkness. Relatively speaking, the 58½ days of cloudiness followed by 58½ days of complete darkness would seem dismal for someone from Earth. Venus could easily bear resemblance to living in a place of outer darkness, as one endures a two-month absence of daylight.

The Spacecraft Revelation of Venus

Space exploration, briefly overviewed in chapter 1, began to take shape in the early 1960s. Space missions divide into by two categories: manned and unmanned programs. Manned flights to orbit the earth or go to the moon are reasonable tasks because of proximity; a safe return for astronauts is highly probable. Interplanetary exploration of planets is best suited for unmanned missions utilizing remote-controlled vehicles, or robotic spacecraft.

---

82 The formula to calculate the duration of a solar day is as follows: Length of Solar Day = Length of Sidereal Day / 1 + (Length of Sidereal Day / Orbital Period of Planet). In a practical sense, the exceedingly slow movement of the sun across the Venusian sky occurs because of two virtually equivalent impulses: the spin of the planet and the coursing of the planet around the sun.

The exploration of outer space through the space programs of the United States and the Soviet Union accomplished important advancements in space technology. Aerospace engineering advanced to the point of placing rocket payloads into orbit reliably and accurately. Launched spacecraft carried well beyond the earth's atmosphere. Equipping these vehicles with active communication subsystems and directional antennas gave the capability of collecting and transmitting data over long distances. The shrouded planet of Venus was soon to be unveiled.

Understanding the environment of our solar system is necessary for successful space travel. As noted in the CMBR discussion, outer space is not a perfect vacuum. The intergalactic, interstellar, and interplanetary mediums contain energized particulate matter. For example, nuclear fusion from the sun brings warmth to our planet. The energy releases the solar wind, a steady stream of charged particles consisting of electrons and protons.

The solar wind expands out in all directions as it moves away from the upper atmosphere of the sun. The energy field forms a bubble-like volume known as the heliosphere, which exists throughout the solar system, stretching beyond the outer planets.[83] The solar wind is a type of plasma that varies in intensity over time. Solar activity such as sunspots and solar flares can affect the amount of emitted radiation that goes into the heliosphere.

Two other concerns of traveling in the interplanetary medium are micrometeoroids and cosmic rays. A micrometeoroid is a dust particle that can physically damage small areas of a

---

83 The launch of NASA space probe Voyager 1 occurred in September of 1977. The spacecraft's mission was to study the outer solar system and to explore deep space. On September 12, 2013, NASA announced that Voyager 1 had left the heliosphere and was moving into interstellar space. The transition occurred in August 2012. NASA, "How Do We Know When Voyager Reaches Interstellar Space?" http://www.jpl.nasa.gov/news/news.php?release=2013-278 (accessed December 18, 2013).

spacecraft due to high velocity impact. Cosmic rays are high-energy particles originating from outside the solar system that travel near the speed of light. Usually in the form of a proton, the charged particle can damage onboard spacecraft processors and cause mission-altering events. Collectively, the solar wind, micrometeoroids, and cosmic rays pose a continual threat to vehicles venturing into outer space.

The United States was the first country to achieve a successful space mission to another planet. On December 14, 1962, NASA's Mariner 2 spacecraft encountered Venus. Attitude control and solar array issues occurred along the way, although none were serious enough to prevent mission success. Mariner 2 flew by Venus at a distance of 21,600 miles and scanned the planet's atmosphere for 42 minutes. Onboard radiometers measured temperatures, while a magnetometer and Geiger-Müller particle tube detected the magnetic field and any radiation belts.

The spacecraft was able to discern the source of the microwave radiation, detected earlier by radio telescopes. It was coming from the surface of the planet, not the clouds. The cloud cover was relatively cool in temperature and projected to extend as high as 40 miles above the ground. Scans made on both the light and dark side of the planet revealed surface temperatures across Venus to be at hundreds of degrees Fahrenheit. Today, we know the mean surface temperature to be near 864°F. The scorching heat will liquefy tin at 450°F, lead at 620°F and zinc at 787°F.

The surface temperature of Venus at a horrific 864°F makes it the hottest planet in the solar system.[84] The global cloud cover forms a greenhouse effect, locking in heat from the carbon dioxide atmosphere. The inferno ensures that "life as we know it" is clearly impossible on the planet. The same cannot be said

---

84 The planet Mercury is an airless terrestrial world that alternately bakes and freezes while orbiting the sun. The sunlit side reaches temperatures of 850°F, but a thermometer would plummet to -300°F on the dark side.

for the afterlife. Prospects for a condemned individual equipped with an immortal spiritual body are not good. Immortality brings durability to resurrected spirits, who like the rich man can endure hot conditions. The globally uniform expanse of heat produces a biblically based, everlasting lake of fire, which maintains a constant temperature both day and night.

The Mariner 2 magnetometer could not discern a magnetic field of any strength in the outer space envelope of Venus. The planet's ability to trap charged particles would be significantly impaired by the lack of a surrounding magnetic force. The Geiger counter could not detect the presence of ionized radiation, giving further evidence to the lack of a magnetosphere.

On Earth, magnetic energy generates from the flow of liquid metal in the outer core. The field strength extends beyond the atmosphere into nearby outer space, forming the magnetosphere. The magnetic field protects the earth from the solar wind and high-energy cosmic rays. The electrons and protons from the sun hit the magnetosphere and form boundary layers (belts) of ionized radiation in nearby outer space. In doing so, the magnetosphere prevents the access of harmful particles to our outer atmosphere.

It would not be until five years later that humanity would achieve another successful encounter with Venus. While not a planned concurrent arrival, Mariner 5 (USA) and Venera 4 (USSR) reached the inner planet just one day apart in October 1967. Venera is the Russian name for Venus. Mariner 5 flew much closer to Venus than the earlier Mariner 2, in the hope of uncovering a magnetic field. The strength of the field found was miniscule, being about 1% of Earth's magnetic field. One notable discovery was high atmospheric pressure.

The Soviet-made Venera 4 main bus carried a probe designed to analyze the atmosphere of Venus during descent. The parachuting capsule transmitted data for over 90 minutes until crushed by the surrounding atmospheric pressure. Direct sensing found the air to consist primarily of carbon dioxide, with atmospheric pressure being 75 to 100 times greater than our own planet. Future missions determined the Venus surface pressure is about 92 times greater than Earth. The high pressure is equivalent to a depth of nearly six-tenths of a mile under the earth's oceans.

Carbon dioxide in the atmosphere normally behaves as a gas at standard temperature and pressure (STP).[85] Pressure and temperature are so extreme on Venus that carbon dioxide is a supercritical fluid, meaning it behaves like both a gas and a liquid. When the gas and liquid phases intermingle, the features become indistinguishable. On a phase diagram, supercritical carbon dioxide lies beyond the boundaries of liquid and gas.[86]

The supercritical carbon dioxide forms a kind of global sea. The expanse retains and transfers heat very efficiently, minimizing day-to-night temperature changes. For this reason, the searing air remains unchanged throughout the extended darkness. The surface is breezeless, with wind speeds averaging less than three miles per hour. The movement allows the transport of dust and small particles across the ground, much like a slow-moving current of water.

The harsh milieu will not affect the health of an individual with an immortal spiritual body. For lost humanity, the foreboding conditions of temperature and pressure speak to the unpleasantness of the planet. The extremely hot, supercritical carbon dioxide feels far heavier than muggy air, but will lack in any water content. Not a single spot on the planet's surface will be able to provide a cool breeze or a breath of fresh air.

Venera 7 and Venera 8 capsules, which visited Venus in 1972 and 1974, respectively, were able to handle the high temperature and atmospheric pressure. Although data

---

85 In chemistry, standard temperature and pressure (STP) is 32°F at an absolute pressure of 14.5 psi (0.987 Atm or 1 bar).

86 In material science, a phase diagram is a graph outlining the effect of pressure and temperature on a substance. The diagram shows dividing lines between solid, liquid and gas.

acquisition was limited, Venera 7 was the first space vehicle to transmit data from the surface of another planet. Engineers believed the vehicle tipped over after landing, misdirecting the antenna signal. Venera 8 was more successful in returning new information, including a ground visibility estimate of about a half mile. The amount of measured light was similar to an overcast day on Earth, making the surface suitable for photography.

Mariner 10, the last spacecraft in the Mariner program, launched in late 1973; the mission objective was an encounter with two planets. There was a flyby of Venus once, followed by a flyby of Mercury three times. The vehicle was the first to use a gravitational slingshot maneuver, employing Venus's gravitational pull to accelerate Mariner 10 toward Mercury. The vehicle's instrumentation suite included an imaging system with twin telescopic cameras and a digital tape recorder. At a distance of 3,600 miles from Venus, Mariner 10 sent back photographs of the cloud-shrouded planet.

Venera 9 and Venera 10 were the beginning of a new generation of Soviet spacecraft, consisting of a two-part orbiter and lander. The design did not employ parachutes or landing rockets because of the high density of the atmosphere. The Venera 9 orbiter was the first vehicle to orbit Venus, while the lander was the first probe to transmit an image from the surface of another world. The orbiter acted as the communications link, relaying data back to the earth. With the cameras of the Venera 9 and 10 landers sitting 3 feet off the ground, each transmitted a clear 180° panorama of the surroundings.

The black and white photography in figure 11 was provided by Venera 9 in October 1975. The images show astonishing detail of a rocky, basalt surface. The Venera 10 landing site, 1,364 miles away, shows a smooth basalt surface. Basalt, a fine-grained, igneous rock formed from the solidification of molten lava, is quite drab compared to other solidified magma like granite, obsidian, or pumice. Basalt soil and rock covers 90% of the Venusian surface.

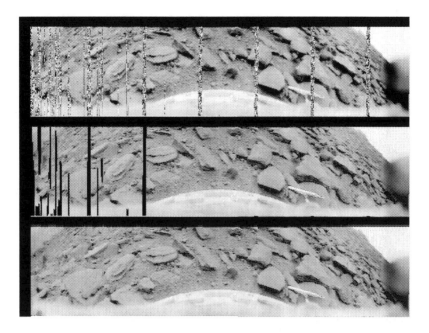

Figure 11
Surface of Venus from Venera 9 Lander

The picture shows an assortment of flat basalt rocks strewn around the landing site. In order to capture a 180-degree wide-angle view, the optical system utilizes a fisheye lens. The fisheye distortion results in a curvature of the image near the edge of the frame. The original photograph at the top includes vertical lines of interference, more extensive on the left side of the image because of bit-stream misalignment as the Venera 9 orbiter moves out of view from the lander. Postprocessing of the successive two lower photographs shows removal of the lines, making for a clearer image. The foot of the lander is visible on the center-right of the picture. In the upper right hand corner, a hazy horizon can be seen in the distance.

It would be hard to believe that technological advancement allows humans to take valid pictures of hell, except for one important fact. It is God's desire for no one to go there. What could be a better deterrent than spacecraft photography of a world that is nothing more than an empty wasteland? Imagine that not one tree, not one plant, not one shrub, not even one blade of grass could exist in this inhospitable environment. No animals, birds, or reptiles would ever be seen in the surroundings. The surface of Venus is covered with gloomy and desolate lava fields, completely lacking in attractiveness and void of any form of life.

Newberry National Volcanic Monument, located south of Bend, Oregon, contains erupted basaltic lavas and obsidian flow. The dry, expansive fields of solidified magma are suggestive of the moon's surface. The only place of interest is the occasional stretch of black, glassy obsidian rock strewn along the ground. Even on a sunny day, the vast areas of basalt formed by volcanism are dreary and oppressive to one's senses. Experiencing the tedium of lava fields on our home planet can provide a sense of concern and urgency in helping people avoid similar conditions on Venus.

In December 1978, four space vehicles, two from the United States and two from the Soviet Union, arrived to investigate Venus. The Russians sent Venera 11 and Venera 12. The spacecraft consisted of a two-part flyby and lander. Unfortunately, the color imaging system failed on each lander when the lens caps did not deploy. Soil sampling failed on each lander because the mechanism did not deposit the soil correctly. However, the spacecraft did record evidence of lightning, and a spectrometer measuring the atmosphere at various wavelengths determined the sky color to be orange-yellow.[87]

Pioneer Venus Orbiter and Pioneer Venus Multiprobe were the two American spacecraft. The Pioneer Venus Multiprobe carried four atmospheric probes. The Pioneer Venus Orbiter

---

87 Due to the Rayleigh scattering, the thick atmosphere of Venus filters out the long wavelength of blue light, leaving an orange-yellow sky. A similar effect occurs on Earth. At sunrise and sunset, the volume of air through which sunlight passes increases as it nears the horizon. The scattering causes the presentation of an orange-red sky.

was designed to make a topographical map of portions of Venus and to record images of the cloud tops. Like its Venera counterparts, the orbiter managed to detect lightning in the atmosphere.

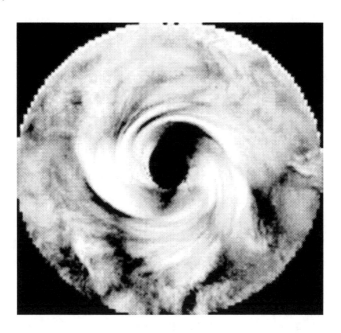

Figure 12
Polar Cloud Top of Venus

The cloud photo-polarimeter from the Pioneer Venus Orbiter created images of the Venus clouds in the near ultraviolet. In figure 12, composite processing of the data provides an intriguing look at an enormous vortex at the North Pole of the planet.[88] With convection driving the atmospheric circulation, equatorial air heated by the sun moves toward the poles. As the currents advance to the higher latitudes, the altitude of the clouds increases. The slowing of the wind speeds and low

---

88 Designation of a North or South Pole should be viewed with caution. Since the solid-body rotation of Venus is retrograde, astronomical usage would label the pole pointing to the south of the Venus orbital plane as the North Pole.

air pressure at the poles combine to form a stunning vortex collapse of the air mass. The upcoming Venus Express mission will provide a more detailed explanation of the thermosphere circulation.

In Revelation 14:11, the Bible states that "the smoke of their torment goes up forever and ever. There is no rest day or night for those who worship the beast and its image and for anyone who receives the mark of its name." The idea of no rest day or night implies afterlife on a planet in rotation about a sun. The smoke of torment going up forever in perdition correlates to the swirling clouds of sulfur dioxide and sulfuric acid, which rise in the Venusian atmosphere prior to vortex entry. Atmospheric vortexes commonly occur in planetary atmospheres, but the ascending of clouds prior to vortex entry is extraordinary.

Pioneer Venus Multiprobe was a bus vehicle designed to inject cone-shaped probes into the atmosphere. One large probe and three smaller probes collected data before impacting the ground. One important finding was the lack of appreciable water in the lower atmosphere. The deficiency of this precious liquid dispels the notion of Venus having clouds similar to Earth. Given the overall planetary conditions, it was not surprising to find the absence of life-giving water. Two of the smaller probes descending on the night side of Venus experienced sparks or flashes of luminosity, indicating a possible presence of lightning.

The Venera 13 and 14 missions of 1981–82 reproduced the efforts of Venera 11 and 12 in trying to obtain color pictures and analyze soil samples. The soil collection mechanism worked well on both landers, with characterization of the basaltic rock being made with an x-ray fluorescent spectrometer. The successful soil analysis was the first-ever on the planet. Venera 13 was able to transmit 360-degree panoramic color photographs, revealing a reddish-brown landscape. Venera 14, some 620 miles from her sister lander, successfully collected similar-type photographs.

Figure 13
Venus Horizon from Venera 13 Lander

The spacecraft view surrounding Venera 13 is shown in a natural perspective. The panoramic image has undergone rectilinear conversion, in order to remove the distortion of the fisheye lens. The black and white photograph shows the toothed-edges of the lander, a ladder-like testing arm, and the semi-circle lens cover. The surrounding area appears to consist primarily of flat, platy rocks and compacted, barren basalt. The visibility extends out to a horizon, perhaps one mile away. A cutout or passageway appears in the distance, along with some indistinguishable small hills.

Venera 13 demonstrates that little or nothing in the environment could hold a person's interest for very long. The lava spew may find initial appeal to a geologist or planetary scientist, but the fascination will wane. The panoramic pictures taken by Venera 14 hundreds of miles away show the same flat rocks and surface. It is very likely the parched and depleted landscape covers the entire globe. Venus is a world gone awry by a runaway greenhouse effect. In looking at the hot volcanic surface, the adjective "hellish" comes to mind.

In the mid-1980s, a clearer understanding of the inner workings of this harsh and uninviting world came into print. Students and serious researchers found important scientific publications such as *The Venus International Reference Atmosphere (Advances in Space Research)* available for study. The book is helpful for modeling and differentiating planetary atmospheres. Earth and Venus each have their own particular atmospheric cycles driven by the sun.

Scientists have characterized the familiar water cycle in the biosphere of Earth. Life-giving water ties the land, oceans, and atmosphere together to form the integrated hydrological cycle. The sun's energy affects the system because water circulates by dropping from clouds to land, flowing out to the ocean, and then evaporating back up to the clouds. The water redistributes from one reservoir to another through natural processes such as precipitation, condensation, evaporation, and runoff. In providing fresh drinking water, the cycle has a direct effect on the quality of human life.

The carbon cycle plays a critical role in the biosphere by providing the capability for the planet to support life. Carbon is prominent in the earth's atmosphere as carbon dioxide. Exchanges between the atmosphere and land, and between the atmosphere and the ocean, facilitate the cycling of carbon through the biosphere. For example, carbon dioxide can leave the atmosphere through plant photosynthesis and enter terrestrial and ocean reservoirs. In recent decades, the burning of fossil fuels has increased the amount of carbon dioxide in the atmosphere, raising concerns about the health of the planet.

On Venus, the sulfur cycle stands out as primary for

the planet. The Venusian world is teeming with hot sulfur, a dominant element found in various forms of sulfur compounds. Sulfur uses the ground, air, and clouds as reservoirs. The chemically active sulfur circulates in the troposphere, moving from the ground to an altitude above the cloud tops. The troposphere divides into four distinct regions, differentiated by altitude. Each zone handles sulfur, or substances containing sulfur, in a different way.[89]

In the Bible, the mention of sulfur (or brimstone) normally attaches to some form of divine retribution and often results in the ruin or death of disobedient people.[90] In the destruction of Sodom and Gomorrah, the Lord rained down fire and sulfur out of heaven (Gen. 19:24; Luke 17:29). In the Apocalypse, the sixth trumpet sends four angels upon the earth to release the three plagues of fire, smoke, and sulfur, killing great multitudes of people (Rev. 9:17–18). In reading Scripture, it is not difficult to associate the presence of sulfur with the punishment of the wicked.

The upper atmosphere of Venus is the "photochemical zone." The layer uses the energy of the sun, along with sulfur dioxide (SO_2), carbon dioxide (CO_2), and trace amounts of water vapor (H_2O) to form sulfuric acid (H_2SO_4) through chemical reaction. The thick clouds masking the surface of Venus are comprised primarily of SO_2 and H_2SO_4. Copious amounts of concentrated H_2SO_4 would rain upon the planet if it were not for the increasing heat at lower elevations.

As the liquid falls from the sky, the high temperature cooks the acid. After dropping about 15 miles, the noxious rain reaches the "evaporation and thermal dissociation zone."

---

89 The four zones of Venus are: (1) the upper atmosphere photochemical zone, (2) the evaporation and thermal dissociation zone, (3) the thermochemistry zone, and (4) the mineral buffering zone near the surface. Grinspoon, *Venus Revealed*, 95–7.

90 Elemental sulfur is a bright yellow crystalline solid at room temperature. When the chemical ignites, it burns with a hot blue flame, producing suffocating fumes of sulfur dioxide.

Here the rain becomes a virga, with the sulfuric acid droplets reaching a boiling point and evaporating during descent. The presence of concentrated sulfuric acid droplets raining from overhead clouds will be a disturbing atmospheric phenomenon to those dwelling on the surface of the planet. Rather than the soothing blue skies of paradisiacal Earth, lost humanity faces an ominous firmament when cast into the lake of fire.

Sulfuric acid is a pungent, clear-yellow chemical that is highly corrosive. One does not encounter the chemical naturally on Earth, due to its great affinity for water. A manufacturer normally creates several grades of H_2SO_4 for application in different industries. Common commercial uses find sulfuric acid in the cells of lead-acid batteries or as an active ingredient in drain cleaners. The chemical is good at dissolving tissue paper, the protein in hair, and various greases that can clog pipes. Concentrated sulfuric acid is unpleasant and quite hazardous, burning the skin to the touch because of its hydroscopic nature.

The "thermochemistry zone" is the next layer of atmosphere lying below the evaporation and thermal dissociation zone at an altitude between 5 and 20 miles above ground. The air ranges in temperature from 200° to 380°F, making the zone chemically active. Lofty temperatures are a catalyst for chemical reactions. High heat increases the molecular motion and the mixing of noxious gases residing in the zone.

Closer analysis of the highly reactive thermochemistry zone requires including data from the Venus Express mission. An important verification of lightning came in 2007 with the detection of whistler-mode waves. A whistler wave is a very low frequency radio wave that can be generated by lightning. The Venus Express whistler waves give credibility to the earlier detection of lightning by the Pioneer and Venera missions, and possible cause to ashen light sightings. Lightning in the

Venusian atmosphere enables important chemical processes to take place that would otherwise not occur.[91]

The lightning events are not the same as on Earth. The perpetual flashes occurring in the orange-yellow sky are likely to be in the clouds and not cloud-to-ground strikes. The thunder bursts from the sky will not bring any rain. Rather, the lightning flashes are the combustion of volatile sulfur compounds in the thermochemistry zone. The idea of "chemical fires" was first proposed during the Venera and Pioneer Venus data evaluation.[92] The penetrating charged particles of the solar wind may serve to ignite hot sulfur compounds in the atmosphere, causing violent chemical reaction.

In Revelation 19:20, the unsaved are thrown into "the lake of fire that burns with sulfur," and in Revelation 21:8, "the lake that burns with fire and sulfur, which is the second death." Burning sulfur is part of the punishment for the unrighteous that have been banished to the lake of fire. The biblical imagery of perdition fits with the ongoing chemical reactions in the atmosphere of Venus. Scientific investigation points to continuous sulfur combustion through lightning events.

At lower altitudes of the troposphere, sound propagation increases dramatically because of the dense medium. Carbon dioxide compacted to a heavy state will markedly strengthen a resonance. The thundering of chemical reactions at great distances can be heard like a powerful nearby storm. The conclusion is clear: individuals banished to Venus will have to live with continuous bursts of thunder and lightning from the burning of sulfur.

The noise may resemble the thunderstorms of Earth, but the rains never come. Below the cloud tops, life-giving water can only

---

91 C.T. Russell et al, "Lightning on Venus Inferred from Whistler-mode Waves in the Ionosphere," *Nature*, 450, No. 7170 (2007): 661–62.

92 Burgess attributes atmospheric flashes from the Pioneer Venus probe to either heat or electrical charges. The reactions involve sulfur compounds above the surface of the planet. Eric Burgess, *Venus: An Errant Twin,* (New York: Columbia University Press, 1985), 95.

be measured in parts per million. Like the rich man in the story of Lazarus, the desire to quench a thirst in the heat will remain with immortal beings. Tasting a drop of water is not possible, but the familiar sounds bringing rain continue as the sulfur burns.

The atmosphere of Venus is primarily composed of carbon dioxide at 96.5%, followed by nitrogen at 3.5%. Trace amounts of sulfur dioxide (150 ppm), argon (70 ppm), water vapor (20 ppm), carbon monoxide (17 ppm), helium (12 ppm), and neon (7 ppm) constitute the remaining air. Gases such as sulfur dioxide (SO_2), as well as hydrogen sulfide (H_2S) and carbonyl sulfide (COS) are present as byproducts of volcanic emission.

The human nose can detect some gases at a level of only a few parts per million. Sulfur dioxide is a gaseous compound that would produce a distinct smell at 150 ppm. SO_2 aligns closely with the trail from a freshly lit match. As a result, the air on Venus will not only be hot and dense but heavy with a foul odor. After His resurrection, Jesus could fully enjoy eating food with His disciples because of a functioning sense of smell. Seeing and smelling the environment is part of the displeasure of spiritual beings banished to Venus.

The final region is the "mineral buffering zone." Located on the ground, it is the hottest area with an air temperature of 864°F; one can assume the same touch temperature for the rocks and soil. Russian scientists published results of spacecraft soil samples from Venera and Vega missions in *Venus Geology, Geochemistry and Geophysics: Research Results from the USSR*. Using x-ray analysis, the scientists were able to quantify the hot magmatic rocks of Venus. Along with eight different types of mineral oxides, the pure elements of sulfur and chlorine were detected in the soil.

A truly comprehensive unveiling of Venus did not happen until the launch of Magellan in the early 1990s. The spacecraft Magellan is named for the sixteenth-century Portuguese explorer Ferdinand Magellan, whose maritime mapping expedition first circumnavigated the earth. Magellan was the first interplanetary mission launched from the Space Shuttle. In May 1989, SS Atlantis deployed the spacecraft with its inertial upper stage (IUS) booster from the cargo bay. The vehicle jetted off to reach Venus in August 1990.

From a highly elliptical polar orbit, Magellan circled the planet every 3 hours and 15 minutes, while using a high-resolution SAR mapping system.[93] With every near pass, Magellan would collect a 16-mile swath of Venus. The vehicle remained essentially fixed in inertial space, while the planet rotated slowly beneath. In order to get complete coverage, Magellan performed three consecutive 243-day (sidereal day) imaging cycles. By September 1992, the mapping of about 98% of the Venusian surface was complete.

The results were outstanding in bringing an up-close and extensive view of relief features and surface configuration. Planetary geologists went on to classify three types of major topographical areas existing on Venus. The first is the mountainous highland terrain, which constitutes about 10% of the surface. Highlands have been compared to the continents of the earth, rising well above the "datum" or zero-elevation level. It is convenient to define a datum, since Venus has no sea.

The second geological zone is the rolling volcanic uplands, making up an impressive 70% of the planet's floor. The vast rolling uplands represent a midlevel transition of terrain from the mountainous highlands to the lowland plains. The smooth lowland plains comprise the remaining 20% of the surface area and compare to the ocean basins of the earth.

---

93 Synthetic aperture radar (SAR) is an active remote sensing and mapping technology. High-energy radio waves emitted from a dish antenna on the spacecraft reflect off the ground and return to the vehicle. During the brief interval, the relative change in satellite location causes a phase shift in the returning radar signal. Onboard computers process the affected signal and produce a high-resolution image. The SAR technique simulates the use of a very large radar antenna. The stored data is transmitted to the ground station on Earth. Joseph A. Angelo, *Encyclopedia of Space and Astronomy*, (New York: Facts on File, 2006), 599.

The continents of Venus have the names Ishtar Terra and Aphrodite Terra. Located at 60°to 70° latitude in the northern hemisphere and about the size of Australia, Ishtar Terra stands out because the continent contains four mountain ranges and an enclosed high plateau. The area might be comparable to the Tibetan Plateau and the surrounding Himalayas. Istar Terra contains the highest mountain range on the entire planet, named Maxwell Montes after the Scottish physicist James Maxwell.

Maxwell Montes reaches an extraordinary elevation of 6.8 miles, which exceeds Mount Everest, the highest mountain on Earth, by over a mile. Due to the elevation, Maxwell Montes experiences a lower atmospheric pressure and is the coolest spot on the planet. Maxwell Montes stands out in altitude and ruggedness because Venus is primarily a low-level world of rolling lava fields.

The second highland terrain, Aphrodite Terra, ranges from 10° N to 20° S of the equatorial region of Venus. Stretching a quarter of the way around the planet, the cumulative land mass approaches the size of Africa. Rugged and highly deformed terrain typifies the region, but the highland area lacks an identifiable mountain range. The complex topography displays mountainous accretions, faults, ridges and troughs cutting across one another.

The rolling volcanic uplands constituting 70% of the surface are host to more than 1500 landforms. More than 100 large volcanoes are 60 miles or more in diameter. Landforms new to geologists necessitated creative nomenclature. Domed mountains with numerous legs around the perimeter were labeled "ticks" because of an insect look. Oval shapes interspersed with a network of fractures resemble a spider's web and were called "arachnoids." Concentric rings of fracture surrounding a depression or a mound were named "corona."

Alpha Regio and Beta Regio are two interesting rolling volcanic upland areas. Alpha Regio sits a mile above the surrounding terrain and it shows rises surrounding what resembles a tile floor. Beta Regio is a prominent upland section displaying spectacular rifts, a feature of shield volcanoes in which a series of radial fissures or large cracks emanates to the flanks. Magma can flow from these cracks, as well as from the summit of the volcano.

The third major geological zone, the lowland plains, constitutes the remaining 20%. The basin generally lacks volcanic and impact-related shapes. Features seen within the lowlands include broad bowl-like depressions and lava channels extending for hundreds of miles. Lowland areas typically manifest as circular depressions or compression-like formations.

Meteorite strikes form large impact craters on Venus. The absence of craters of less than one mile in diameter is attributable to small meteorites being fragmented and burning up in the dense atmosphere. The edges of many craters are amazingly sharp, inferring limited surface erosion and little to no plate tectonics. The random spatial distribution of the young-looking craters implies a global cataclysmic resurfacing of the planet in the last billion years or less.

What is to be made of these lava formations from the perspective of Venus becoming a place of perdition? Throughout the global volcanic landscape, residences have been naturally prepared for those cast into the lake of fire. The only requirement for a banished spiritual being will be to provide housing. Geologists researching images of the Venusian plains identify channels and various conduits emplaced by lava flow. The fields built by volcanism are home to countless numbers of lava tubes, lava caves, vertical rift caves, and miscellaneous fractures or openings on the flanks of lava channels.[94]

---

94 The volcanism on the surface of Venus is teeming with cavernous places such as lava tubes and lava caves. Ronald Greeley, *Lava Tubes in the Solar System,* (6th International Symposium on Vulcanospeleology, Tempe, AZ: Arizona State University Planetary Geology Group, 1992), 228.

Lava tubes are the most extensive type of dwelling. The formation of a lava tube begins when molten lava leaves the area of eruption in a flowing channel. As the hot lava flows over long distances, it tends to solidify around the exterior because the surrounding air is cooler than the lava. The process creates an insulating barrier for the molten lava to advance in the center. The progression leaves open interior spaces because the lava supply continues to flow after the exterior has solidified. The final form is a cylindrical cavity built from solid walls of basalt, shaping the habitation.

Spiritual beings sent to the lake of fire will reside in some form of encrusted lava dwelling. The following table is purely hypothetical, being based on Satan and his demonic army having first choice of a Venusian abode.

Reference	Immortal Entity	Planet Location
Rev. 19:20	The Beast and False Prophet	Ishtar Terra
Rev. 20:10	Satan	Maxwell Montes
Rev. 20:14	Death	All of Venus
Rev. 20:14	Hades (demons)	Ishtar Terra Aphrodite Terra Alpha Regio Beta Regio
Rev. 20:15	Anyone not found written in the book of life.	Rolling Uplands Lowland Plains

Table 2
Hypothetical Dispersion of Beings Cast into the Lake of Fire

It would not be out of character for Satan to occupy the highest elevation on Venus, in order to have the best position on the worst of terrestrial planets. His pride led to his fall, and now it works to secure the highest mountain in this desolate world. The soaring peak of Maxwell Montes serves as the extraordinary location for the self-serving devil. The high ground brings seclusion and a sense of superiority, while offering slightly cooler temperatures and lower pressures. The better-quality piece of land does not mean Satan escapes the emotional distress of his deportation.

The devil, the beast, and the false prophet suffer torment day and night in the lake of fire. The suffering of Satan primarily relates to his deportation and loss of authority. The devil has no need to control a demonic army because spiritual warfare with God, the holy angels, and all of humanity has drawn to a close. With the spiritual domain of Hades having been exiled from the earth, the devil's influential rule is gone. The subordinates in his militia are scattered around the Venusian globe. At the end of the age, he suffers final defeat, though he has taken many souls with him.

The fallen angels of the spiritual domain of Hades will share the same fate of Satan at the time of judgment. These malevolent beings have tempted, attacked, oppressed, hindered, and deceived multitudes of people throughout human history. Sent to Venus, the creatures are likely to occupy the higher ground below Satan. Once Ishtar Terra and Aphrodite Terra fill, they will move to inhabit the other highland areas of Alpha Regio and Beta Regio. Death is also thrown into the lake of fire. Death was first a permanent biological cessation of all vital functions and now has become a spiritual condition. It is a state spread out over the entire planet.

Unrighteous humanity will undergo a resurrection of condemnation. Immortal human spirits face eternal ruin in areas outside the mountainous highland terrain. The lower elevations of the planet are reserved for lost humanity and are less likely to contain demonic spirits. Revelation 21:8 tells of the faithless, the polluted, the murderers, the fornicators, and all liars having a place in the lake of fire and sulfur, which is the second death. The immortal spiritual bodies of unsaved people will be transported to Venus by an angelic workforce under orders to place persons in specific lava caves.

Untold numbers of angelic beings, who normally serve as messengers of God and protectors of God's people, will be employed in the relocation effort. Jesus addresses the final judgment in Matthew 13:49–50, telling the audience, "So it will be at the end of the age. The angels will come out and separate the evil from the righteous and throw them into the furnace of fire, where there will be weeping and gnashing of teeth."

Angels and immortal spiritual bodies have amazing durability to face the harshness of interplanetary space. A pressurized space suit containing an oxygen supply and environmental control system is not necessary. When Jesus ascends through the clouds in Acts 1:9, there is no mention of having to wear a protective garment. Without any additional outfitting, the Lord made His journey through the upper atmosphere and into the vastness of outer space, toward the celestial heaven. One can believe angels and unsaved immortal spirits travel just as safely through the darkness of space toward another planet.

Once beyond the exosphere of the paradisiacal Earth, the lost person will be able to look back and see the "Blue Marble," that famous 1972 photograph of the planet taken by astronauts during the Apollo 17 mission. In space, the crystalline sphere of Earth contains beautiful blue ocean waters, bright white clouds and sandy-colored continents to form a large, stunning blue marble. The spectacle is a last look at what could have been home. The stars of the Milky Way will be numerous and bright during the interplanetary journey. As the trek approaches the clouds of Venus, individuals get one final clear view of the sun and surrounding galaxy.

After dropping into the lower atmosphere of Venus, the individual will arrive at a repulsive environment shaped by volcanism. Due to the rest mass of the immortal spiritual body, the person will be subject to the same gravitational laws as the mortal physical body. He or she will be locked into the Venusian world. Gravity acts upon all inhabitants, so it will be impossible to "break free" from the grip of the planet. The angel will deliver the individual to a lava dwelling on the Venusian surface, which can house several banished people.

Each person will appear as an independent, self-sufficient, and responsible adult who will coexist in a shared space. The members of a cave dwelling are likely to have similar cultural backgrounds. One fissure may have individuals from North America, while another cave has inhabitants from Europe, and still another from Asia or Africa. People living on the earth during a certain period of history will likely be grouped with people who lived during or near the same time. Conversation will flow freely within the group. Individuals are able to relate his or her life stories and circumstances to one another.

Lava tubes providing housing are not necessarily in close proximity to one another. Cavernous places exist everywhere, and occupied hollows may be spaced apart, perhaps by a few miles. The Venus landscape does not facilitate venturing out on long field trips to find others. Getting your bearings straight on this vast, barren and generally unchanging terrain is no small task. Because the upper-level clouds whisk by, a hazy sun-shape may be evident from time to time. Since the position of the sun changes quite slowly over 58½ days, the faint sun outline can provide some directionality.

Recent Missions and Summary

Launched in November 2005, Venus Express was one of the most successful pursuits to our neighboring planet. After eight years of data collection, the European Space Agency concluded the mission in December 2014. The spacecraft examined the dynamics of the atmosphere and the chemical interactions near the ground. Data from the spacecraft has given additional supporting evidence for atmospheric lightning.

Recent information also suggests the planet is still geologically active, with reporting of active volcanoes on the planet being as recent as April 2010.[95]

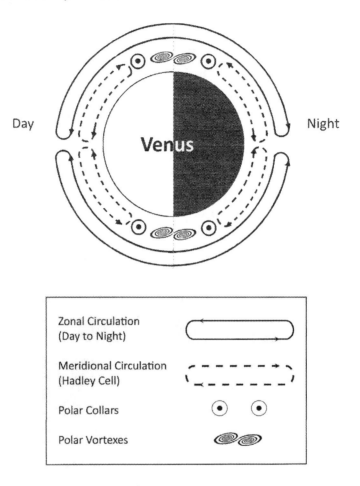

Figure 14
Zonal and Meridional Circulation

By operating from a highly elliptical orbit, Venus Express could study the mechanism behind the super rotation in

---

95 New York Times, "Spacecraft Spots Active Volcanoes on Venus," http:// www.nytimes.com/ 2010/ 04/10/science/space/10venus.html (accessed June 17, 2013).

the upper atmosphere. As shown in the pictorial of Venus, the behavior of winds varies at different altitudes with the atmospheric circulation dividing into two distinct strata.[96] The upper altitude contains the zonal layer, which is responsible for the day to night circulation in the thermosphere. At this level, the wind can average rates of 225 mph below 50° latitude. The super-rotation speed of the winds approaches sixty times the rotation rate of the planet. As the zonal winds move toward the poles, the momentum decreases by almost two-thirds.

The second layer of circulating wind below the zonal winds is the meridional, which is called a Hadley cell. The earth exhibits a similar flow in the troposphere. George Hadley did research in the eighteenth century on atmospheric circulation patterns that sustain the trade winds. Above the winds of the tropics are closed-loop, circulating patterns called Hadley cells. On Venus, similar type air masses arise at the equator and move north-south (along the meridian). The wind speeds are much slower than the upper zonal flow, with the Hadley cell contacting the polar collars at approximately 60° latitude.

The cold collars contain a dense, relatively cool air mass, which acts as a barrier. The slight obstruction by the polar collars is responsible for the climb of the zonal winds approaching the polar regions. Prior to entering the circulation path of the vortex, the clouds ascend for several miles in distinct fashion to form a polar ring cloud (see figure 12).

The final atmospheric constituent is a pair of vortexes at the north and south poles. The vortexes are much larger in diameter than Earth-size tropical hurricanes. The periphery of the vortex begins with the escalated zonal air, which funnels down into the central, low-pressure area. Each vortex is complex, containing two eyes. The swirling collapse of the vortexes can penetrate up to thirty miles, extending to the base of the cloud formation.

---

96 Hakan Svedhem, Dmitry V Titov, Fredric W. Taylor, and Olivier Witasse, "Venus as a More Earth-like Planet," *Nature*, 450, No. 7170 (2007): 629–32.

The detailed findings of Venus Express explain the meteorological reason for the ascension of zonal air. The high-speed air mass lifts over the polar collars in approaching the vortexes. The recent mission answers the "why" for the 1978 Pioneer Venus discovery of rising clouds in the single large vortex. The acquired data brings scientific explanation to Revelation 14:11, where the smoke of torment continues upward forever and ever for those in perdition. The smoke is essentially the swirling atmospheric cloud-cover of sulfuric acid and sulfur dioxide.

Two other missions exploring the inner planet are the Akatsuki Venus Orbiter (AVO) and the Venus Spectral Rocket (VeSpR) experiment. The Japan Aerospace Exploration Agency (JAXA) operates the AVO. The spacecraft reached Venus in December 2010, but a failure in the bipropellant engine occurred during the planned orbit insertion. After discovering the spacecraft in safe-hold, the team reactivated the onboard systems. After five years in a solar orbit, JAXA placed the AVO in an elliptical orbit around Venus. Planned science operations began in April 2016.

The VeSpR experiment launched on 26 November 2013 from White Sands, N.M. using a telescope mounted inside a suborbital rocket. The payload was successfully retrieved from the upper atmosphere for data review. Sensing was also done on the Hubble Space Telescope. Since Earth's atmosphere absorbs ultraviolet, the UV from Venus cannot be observed from the ground. The VeSpR test will measure the ratio of deuterium (heavy hydrogen) to hydrogen. Theoreticians are analyzing the data, in order to determine if water once existed on the surface in a moist greenhouse, or whether small amounts have always been locked in the upper atmosphere.

Closing this section is a list of the orbital and physical characteristics of Venus. The scientific findings of the inner planet correlate directly to the noted biblical passages describing hell and the lake of fire. The connection to perdition extends into the vignette of the next chapter.

- The period after sunset or before dawn brings viewing times when Venus can be seen from heaven on Earth. The righteous can look upon the celestial body and be reminded of the banishment and distress of the unrighteous (Rev. 14:10 and Isa. 66:24a).
- The average surface temperature of 864°F produces the hottest environment in the solar system, with the day-to-night transition being isothermal. The unchanging temperature is indicative of the unquenchable fire of hell (Matt. 3:12 and Mark 9:43).
- The interplanetary transfer is a voyage into the outer darkness of outer space. Upon arrival on Venus, the 58½ days of continuous night brings a sense of outer darkness to spiritual beings that are familiar with the day/night cycle of the earth (Matt. 8:12 and 25:30).
- The volatile, sulfur-based compounds, which continually ignite through evidence of lightning in the atmosphere of Venus, create a lake of fire that burns with sulfur (Rev. 19:20 and 21:8).
- Due to the cold temperature obstruction of the polar collars, the zonal airflow ascends, causing a lifting of the acid clouds at the north and south poles. The unusual phenomenon can be understood as the rising smoke of torment going up forever and ever (Rev. 14:11a).
- Having no rest day or night (Rev. 14:11b) and to be in torment day and night (Rev. 20:10) occurs on a rotating planetary body orbiting the sun. Unrest and torment can come from loud and continuous chemical reactions (lightning) in the sky.
- The vignette in the next chapter addresses additional temperament and emotional issues resulting from being

sequestered to Venus. These conditions correlate to scriptural references.

The highlights from the chapter connect Venus, or a planet similar to Venus, directly to perdition. The scientific evidence draws initially from the unaided eye. Telescopes and space probes gather data for surface temperature, orbital and rotation period, chemical makeup and meteorology. The technical findings assimilate to describe an unpleasant environment for unsaved spiritual beings after final judgment with each discovery having a direct correlation to passages in the Bible. The idea of the planet Venus being the eternal place of banishment substantiates through empirical evidence from the sciences.

CHAPTER 6

Rational Punishment

Therefore the wicked will not stand in the judgment,
nor sinners in the congregation of the righteous;
for the Lord watches over the way of the righteous,
but the way of the wicked will perish.

Psalms 1:5–6

Dispensational premillennialism is one type of eschatological belief where Jesus Christ will return to Earth to produce a visible kingdom. His sovereign rule and reign will be on a renewed planet for a period of one thousand years. Those who return with Christ and the remaining people living in the world following the tribulation period will coexist in a theocratic kingdom of joy, peace, and justice. The passage in Revelation 20:6 tells of the blessed individuals who are resurrected in order to reign on the earth as priests of God.

Satan is bound in Hades for one thousand years during the dispensation, but is released from the pit at the end of the duration. His wickedness remains unchanged following the lengthy imprisonment. Amazingly, the devil is once again able to deceive nations around the globe and gather them to fight against the saints. The aggression ends when God comes to the rescue and stops the advance of the marching army (Rev. 20:7–9). The failed rebellion results in the devil's deportation to the lake of fire.

At this stage, the underworld of Hades empties out, and the unrighteous that have lived throughout history will come before the throne of God. During the final judgment, various books will be opened containing the life summary of every person. A review of thoughts, words, and deeds will be made and weighed against existing law or moral code. At the end of the proceeding, the book of life opens to determine a person's eternal status. If one's name is not found in the book, the individual will face the final sentence of the lake of fire.

Judgment Day did not go well for six men in the following vignette. As foretold by the scriptures, sentencing results in condemnation and departure from the presence of the Lord. Removal from the earth and relocation to the lake of fire is the final phase of the plan. Being exiled to a planet such as Venus is a terrible fate that results in lost people being sequestered to an undesirable world.

Six Men in a Lava Tube

The end of the age brought the Second Coming of Christ in 2145, resulting in a one-thousand-year reign on the earth. The great white throne judgment took place in 3145, following the end of Satan's final rebellion and his being cast into the lake of fire. The year is 3165. Twenty years have passed since these six men were transported to Venus and dropped off in a lava tube in the Venusian lowlands. The cave is about 200 miles north of the Venera 9 landing site.

Three of the men were boomers, part of the United States baby boom generation, living on Earth between 1950 and 2040. The other three American men lived between 2050 and 2145, experiencing a host of tumultuous events recorded in the book of Revelation, chapters 6 through 18. The tribulation period (2138–2145) brings many plagues upon the earth, including the aforementioned demonic locust attack.

Bob, Larry, Roy, Steve, Eric, and Jeff live together in a lava cave. The following is some personal history on each individual:

- Bob, a physical therapist from Bridgeport, Connecticut, died in 2037 at age 84.
- Larry was a regional sales manager from Fort Wayne, Indiana, who died in 2027 at age 75.
- Roy died in 2144 at age 81 and had been a construction worker from Sacramento, California.
- Steve was a lawyer from Houston, Texas, who died in 2141 at age 76.
- Eric a high school English teacher from Chicago, Illinois, died in 2029 at age 79.
- Jeff, who died in 2143 at age 88, was a security guard from Baltimore, Maryland.

The character of these immortal spiritual beings has not changed from the corporeal state. The Holy Spirit did not convict the soul of each during their time on the earth. Unwillingness to experience salvation resulted in these six men retaining a sinful nature at death. The soul substance carries the traits of the individual into Hades, violating the divine intention. At final judgment, the soul resurrects to an immortal spiritual body with the same disposition. Estranged from God, the men are banished from Earth and placed together on Venus.

Our story opens as the men consider making a run from the lava tube. Since arriving on the planet two decades earlier, the men have endured boredom and monotony day after day— feelings that demonstrate the enigmatic "worm never dies" found in Mark 9:48 and Isaiah 66:24b. The overcast skies and the barren terrain of Venus offer little aesthetic pleasure to an immortal spiritual body capable of enjoying so much more.

The anguish of their existence is attested to by the smoke of torment, endlessly rising, as referred to in Revelation 14:11. Members of the lava tube regularly experience tormenting restlessness. This restlessness pushes the longing to leave, but negotiating the unfamiliar terrain and the ever-present, loud chemical reactions in the sky drives the desire to leave the cave dwelling together. But they cannot agree on when and how. The difficulty appears to lie in their limited ability to navigate by day and the complete inability to navigate by night. In actuality, the real problem is that there in is no escape from Venus.

Several passages in Matthew warn that there will be "weeping and gnashing of teeth" in perdition.[97] Luke 13:28 reveals the weeping and gnashing is a result of missing out on the kingdom of God. The passage in Luke implies being able to physically identify people who have been admitted to the kingdom of God, prior to departing for the lake of fire. Weeping is an expressive state of grief, sorrow, or sadness. On the other hand, gnashing of teeth is an attitude of anger, irritation, and resentment. Having an unemotional disposition toward missing out and ending up in difficult circumstances can occur as well.

Bob and Larry have been distressed since their arrival on Venus. Their despondency vacillates between shedding dry tears in the corner of the hollow and no expression at all. While hell is not a good place, each man is against the idea of leaving. Feelings of hopelessness keep Bob and Larry "safe" in the cave.

Expressing a counter temperament, Steve and Roy are outraged about having been cast into the lake of fire, occasionally gritting their teeth in anger. They have anxiously scouted the terrain during the extended daylight. At the next opportunity, they are ready to leave the cave.

Eric and Jeff have not expressed a lot of emotion over the years. Clearly, Venus is not a good place, but it seems better

---

97 The Matthew passages are 8:12; 13:42; 13:50; 22:13; 24:51; and 25:30. Coogan, *New Oxford Annotated Bible*, 18, 28, 42, 47, 48 [New Testament].

than the confines of Hades. Maintaining an even temperament and trying to be helpful, they spend their energy encouraging Bob and Larry in times of depression. Eric and Jeff have entertained the idea of leaving, but have not made up their minds.

Twenty-five Earth-days into the outer darkness of the Venusian night finds our little group sitting around a large natural basalt rock near the entry of their lava cave. The stone has become the centerpiece of the communal setting. Steve, who is annoyed and on his soapbox about leaving the lava tube, comments flippantly,

"Okay, sports fans, are we ready to blow this pop stand? We've been hanging around this lousy cave for twenty years and it's getting pretty mind-numbing."

Eric responds, "And where, may I ask, do you think we should go? The horizon is blurred by clouds and that disgusting lava field looks the same in every direction."

"Well, we can start traveling due East at dawn with the light at our back," Steve offered. "I'm sure we'll hit upon something— maybe another cave with people we can talk to."

Bob joins the conversation, but can only muster sadness, "But the angel who dropped me off here said not to leave the cave. I'm sure you were told the same thing."

Roy is incensed. "And what do you think your reward is going to be for following those instructions? Besides, since when are you into obeying God? We need to stop this idle chatter and leave this place."

"But wait a minute, Roy," Jeff countered. "Those grotesque demon locusts could be out there—the same ones that tormented us on the earth. What if we run across those creatures?"

Roy picks up a flat basalt rock. "Then it's payback time! I was stung by one of those beasts and suffered for months. I'm ready to deal with them now." He breaks the rock in two to emphasize his determination.

"Payback?" Jeff scoffs at Roy. "Using what? Your bare hands? Those creepy things are big and fast. We need weapons and we can't make any, at least not here."

With remorse in his voice, Larry adds his piece, "We should have repented in our lifetime, trusting Jesus Christ as our Lord and Savior. None of us would be here if we had made the right decision."

Steve is irritated. "Are you going to bring up that same old stuff again? It's over with now. We made up our minds back on Earth. Let's deal with reality and stop feeling sorry about the past."

"The reality is," Eric responds, "that we are bored out of our minds. I now understand what was meant by 'where their worm never dies.'"[98] He surrounds his words with air quotes. "We just sit here day in and day out with absolutely nothing to do, except continually lament our situation."

Steve is angry. "That's precisely why I'm trying to get us out of here! We can keep ourselves busy by scouring the planet for other people and places. We don't sleep; we never get tired. What's to stop us from succeeding?"

What's your idea of success, Steve?" Eric asks curiously. "Finding other people on Venus who are suffering like us? So what? We listen to their stories and suffer with monotony again in a few months?"

Larry asks the others, "Do you remember seeing the beautifully restored Earth on Judgment Day? Who wants to spend time walking through these volcanic fields feeling heartbroken?"

"Well, it sure is better on the surface of this planet than in Hades," Jeff retorted. "I still remember the fear, the total darkness, and the lack of any human contact in that solitary confinement."

Roy concurs that this is a better place, relatively speaking.

---

98 Coogan, *New Oxford Annotated Bible*, 1072 [Old Testament], 75–6 [New Testament].

"It was hard for me to breathe down there. At least the stench is not as bad in this place—well, except when the lightning strikes nearby."

Bob agrees. "The lightning flashes and thundering sounds from those chemical storms are really intimidating. I don't want to be near any of those flare-ups."

Eric sums up the conversation. "Sounds like we're lacking a consensus on leaving, Steve. If you and Roy really want to go, you could make a run for another cave in the morning."

Steve concedes, "I can't see Roy and me leaving just yet. It's just too risky to go out there with only two guys. We'll just have to wait here and talk about it another time."

"Steve, if I decide to join you and Roy in the future," Jeff offers, "the group would be evenly divided. A team of three men should be safe enough. We can always come back."

Eric is dubious. "I'm not sure if or when you guys would ever get back. The landscape is too confusing."

"Hey, Jeff, maybe you can pray about it!" Roy says sarcastically. "In the meantime, I'll be leaving when Steve decides to go."

This brief scene depicts the frustration and distress of being separated from God for an eternity. Perdition is a rational and coherent form of afterlife existence. It is not a black hole or unimaginable state of being, as many people perceive. Although a dramatization of futuristic events, this vignette could actually play out in eternity.

The immortal spiritual body is durable enough to endure the harsh Venusian environment. The question becomes, "Where will this group end up that will improve their situation?" Further, what benefit is there to having eternally enduring features and ground mobility on a dismal planet? True escape is impossible because gravity has your spiritual body bound to a lifeless lava field. You cannot break away. By ignoring the call to salvation, one risks an eternal future of banishment and frustration on

Venus. It is a road to death and destruction that this book is trying to help people avoid.

The antithetical state is everlasting life, which our heavenly Father originally intended for these men. Second Peter 3:9 tells the reader that God is "not wanting any to perish, but all to come to repentance." The celestial heaven is completely counter to a cavity in the center of the earth. And after final judgment, heaven on Earth will be far more glorious than the volcanic nothingness of Venus. Heaven is not only God's home but is a place of supreme beauty and harmonious living. Blessed by the presence of friends, family, angels, and God, paradise completely lacks in pain, evil, or monotony.

Every reader of the Bible receives instruction to test the spirits, in order to assess the teaching and any false or misleading doctrine (1 John 4:1–6). It is the Holy Spirit who leads and guides every individual in truth. People of faith have a responsibility to pray about a message heard in relation to Scripture, and then to discern whether the presentation is rightful and honoring of God. This book may seem unconventional in comparison to other Christian literature; it may be far reaching with regard to disclosure. Yet, the concepts provided here support the existence of hell and the necessity of finding salvation and security with the Creator.

Comparing Hades to Venus

The following table summarizes the information presented in the book and draws a distinction between Hades and hell/lake of fire.

Item	Hades	Hell/Lake of Fire
Duration	The present day until final judgment	For an eternity
Location	In the center of planet Earth	On the surface of planet Venus
Afterlife State	Human soul	Immortal spiritual body
Confinement	Inner core voids	Lava tubes
Human Companionship	Possible	More certain
Confined Demons	In chains	Scattered over the surface of Venus
Suffering	Separation, loss, and anguish	Separation, loss, and anguish

Table 3
Comparison of Hades and Hell/Lake of Fire

Personal suffering will occur whether in Hades or on the surface of Venus. The Bible seems to indicate some individuals may suffer more than others. A greater condemnation (Matt. 23:14), light or severe beatings (Luke 12:47–48), and just penalties for disobedience (Heb. 2:2–3) can substantiate degrees of punishment. Just as isolation for notorious criminals is common in today's prison system, solitary confinement is one likely form of discipline for individuals in the afterlife. Human companionship is a privilege that can be removed in both the mortal and immortal existence.

Even before the Day of Judgment, the guilty person will likely know the extent of his or her sin. Two biblical examples attribute knowledge and awareness to the departed soul. First, in the earlier parable of the rich man and Lazarus, Jesus makes clear that the rich man knew the reason for his suffering. The rich man did not have to wait until final judgment in order to understand the basis for his separation from Abraham's bosom. He knew the extent of his sin and the punishment set in place.

Second, we can examine the story of King Saul's visit to the medium of Endor in 1 Samuel 28:3–19. Samuel, who is summoned by the medium, is looked upon as being able to provide understanding and direction to Saul. Samuel tells Saul that he has lost favor with God and that he and his sons will die the next day in battle with the Philistines. The outcome of the conflict turns out exactly as Samuel predicts. The soul of Samuel speaks with prudence and knowledge in a precarious situation. It is likely that his greater understanding extends beyond Saul's immediate problem to encompass himself and his standing with God.

Some theological approaches to personal eschatology believe guilty souls do not find out the full measure of sin until the white throne judgment. This would leave the lake of fire as the place for administering different levels of discipline. Solitary confinement can be achieved in any number of locations. The isolation can occur in a cave or fissure but may be a temporary condition. The inner planet is a difficult enough environment without having to suffer alone eternally. As one can glean from the lava tube narrative, six men keeping each other company already experience sufficient sorrow.

The lava tube vignette provides a sufficiently rational view of potential conditions for lost people. The visualization helps to refute notions of annihilationism and universalism. When Christians buy into these ideas, they believe God will act differently toward the lost than what Scripture teaches. To those without faith in God, to those who have heard and rejected the gospel, to those who think the Bible is a work of fiction; well, this is perhaps an important writing to consider. As a familiar celestial object, the planet Venus presents a scientific and scripturally based physical location for hell.

Is Venus the only available location in the entire cosmos for sending spiritual beings into exile? The answer is probably not, but there would not be a theological or scientific reason for God needing to choose another planet. A surrogate for the lake of fire can situate on one of many exoplanets outside the solar system. As mentioned earlier, extrasolar planets are innumerable in quantity, with the discovery of new exoplanets continuing at a rapid pace. The search focuses on bodies in the habitability zone, which have possible Earth-like features.[99]

Astronomers give study to exoplanets that can possibly support life. These remote objects can be gauged in size for comparison to Earth or Venus. Can a newly discovered exoplanet turn out to have the same environmental conditions as Venus? It is hard to know. The great distances of space preclude close environmental analysis of the planetary bodies. Still, another hot, cloud-covered, inhospitable world filled with lava fields and a fiery, sulfuric atmosphere is very probable in the expanse of the universe.

In order for condemned spiritual beings to reach an exoplanet, it may require travel through a wormhole. Immortal spiritual bodies having physical mass are restricted from traveling at the speed of light. While a surrogate Venus is

---

99 It has been estimated that 22% of sun-like stars in our galaxy harbor Earth-size planets in habitable zones. National Academy of Sciences of the United States of America Proceedings, "Prevalence of Earth-size Planets Orbiting Sun-like Stars," http://www.pnas.org/content /110/48/19273 (accessed December 10, 2013).

likely to be coursing around a star many light-years beyond our solar system, traversing there expediently would require a wormhole in space-time. The idea of wormholes acting as a time travel conduit finds respectability in astrophysics. The original concept of a hypothetical passage originates in the 1935 work of Einstein and Nathan Rosen.

Analysis in later years showed a wormhole to be unstable, lacking the ability to stay open long enough to allow passage. Further research in the late 1980s led physicists to conclude that wormholes could stay open, if placed in a region of space-time containing matter with negative energy density. Negative mass and negative energy is a hypothetical, "less than nothing" condition, but quantum mechanics suggests such regions of space do exist. So travel through a wormhole to reach an exoplanet of exile is not out of the realm of possibility.

Final Thoughts

Twenty years is a long time in the personal history of an individual. Yet, it was for more than twenty years that agnostic and atheistic thinking permeated my life. The state of my disbelief began as a late teen. If memory serves me correctly, it came after becoming angry and disillusioned with God. Falling away from the faith seems to happen a lot that way.

People have a degree of childhood faith and then smack! Something bad happens to upset our fragile lives. A disappointment can overwhelm us. A family member or friend becomes gravely ill. Death takes away a loved one. We become aware of innocent people suffering inexcusably and horribly. And God gets the blame. He moves from being a spiritual acquaintance to an adversary, and then from being an adversary to nonexistent.

A hard outer shell forms over the years, closing off the spiritual. I took a cynical, even caustic approach toward religious conviction. If you were a negative individual in matters of religion and faith, you would have enjoyed keeping my company. Wanting little or nothing to do with church, I considered attendees to be emotionally weak, deceived, or, at best, in need of something to do on Sunday. A Christian stepping forward and witnessing to me was not only wasting his or her time, but also exposing a major character flaw. To put it bluntly, I was lost, as lost as a goat in a snowstorm.

How God was able to achieve a 180-degree turn in my belief system remains a bit of a mystery. It was after my fortieth birthday, venturing through post-divorce dating, that I got together with a former girlfriend. She had the Lord in her life and convinced me to reevaluate my spiritual condition. Her pastor went on to recommend a local church to attend in the area where I lived. It was only a few short weeks before I began driving there for Sunday service.

After a few weeks of listening to good sermons, watching uninhibited expressiveness in worship and listening to people speak in tongues, I became convinced of the reality of God. Beholding the power of the Holy Spirit at work in a Pentecostal church converted this engineer-type, who generally needed firsthand witnessing of spiritual gifts as evidence of a supreme being. But what kept me growing in my faith was far deeper.

It was forgiveness. How could God forgive me for all the years of irreverence, profanity, unbelief, and immorality? Wasn't there a price to pay to get into heaven after all that I had done? Then I remembered. Jesus Christ paid the price for me. He paid through one of the most excruciating and painful ways of dying, his own death on a cross. This realization keeps me on my knees daily.

An essential purpose of this writing is to understand the love God has for every individual person on the planet. The fire and brimstone of Venus were prepared for the devil and his angels, not for human beings. To make a way for salvation, God sent His only begotten son, Jesus Christ, into the world to be our Lord and Savior. His sacrificial life was exemplified by love, compassion, and forgiveness for others. Romans 5:6–8 reads,

> For while we were still weak, at the right time Christ died for the ungodly. Indeed, rarely will anyone die for a righteous person—though perhaps for a good person someone might actually dare to die. But God proves his love for us in that while we still were sinners Christ died for us.

The passage begins by uncovering the anemic state of humanity. We are spiritually disenfranchised from God and powerless to help ourselves. Proven unable to resist sin and to keep the righteous requirements of the law, we need help in order to be reconciled to God. A righteous or good person, one who is truly moral and blameless, is difficult to find. Not even the best people are consistently pure in thought and deed.

It is difficult to overcome the indulgences of the world and the natural tendency to center on self. An intercessor, a go-between, someone who could be perfect on our behalf, is necessary to rectify the estrangement. Having an upright and innocent character, Jesus kept Himself unblemished in the world and was sinless throughout the entire course of his eventful life and ministry.

Foreshadowing the surrogate nature of the sin sacrifice is the account of Israelite worship in the Old Testament. Presenting an annual offering of bulls, rams, goats, and other animals to the temple priest was a necessity for right standing. The burnt offerings of blameless creatures illustrate the need for vicarious blood atonement before God, an atonement that Jesus willingly made on our behalf. His suffering and death in our stead compensates for every person's wrongdoing. Continuing in Romans 5:9–11, the scripture reads:

> Much more surely then, now that we have been justified by his blood, will we be saved through

him from the wrath of God. For if while we were enemies, we were reconciled to God through the death of his Son, much more surely, having been reconciled, will we be saved by his life. But more than that, we even boast in God through our Lord Jesus Christ, through whom we have now received reconciliation.

Justification is a reckoning or counting of a person as righteous. It brings God together with those who have previously been distant from Him. Age, dress, physical features, or the social and financial standing of an individual are of no concern. The atonement of Christ brings deliverance to all. God and the believer come to a final resolution concerning sin and salvation. The rescue of our soul means keeping us from Hades. This change in status moves the person from a position of being condemned to being blameless. It removes the penalty for sin and eliminates any chance of facing eternal banishment.

Who do you consider an adversary or enemy? Do you have strong feelings about someone you see regularly or a person from your past? Perhaps it is an annoying coworker, or a neighbor, or an official in government who holds different political views. What group upsets you? Is it Al-Qaeda or the Islamic State (ISIL)? These international terrorist-based organizations are responsible for the death of tens of thousands. Would you die for such people? Would you say, "No, don't put that terrorist to death for what he did. Take my life instead and let him go?" The very thought is ridiculous.

Yet, the idea fully illustrates what Jesus Christ did for us. His sacrificial death on the cross at Calvary took place while we were enemies of God, who willingly oppose Him. Not only does God remove the punishment for sin, but He adds a great deal of joy to life through daily fellowship with the Holy Spirit. A renewed mind and a changed life, as well as faith, trust, and peacefulness of heart, are all part of the gifting of the atonement. The grace of God pours into our lives in order to sanctify us. And in the end, God gives eternal life and the ability to dwell in His presence. This is the incalculable and unconditional love of God.

The real authority of the gospel message is in Jesus getting up out of the grave. The legitimacy of Christianity lies in the power of the resurrection. If Christ is not raised, our faith is in vain (1 Cor. 15:4). Without the resurrection, Christian preaching and belief is meaningless. A significant portion of the New Testament centers on this critical historical fact. The empty tomb, the documented appearances before hundreds of people, and the testimony and martyrdom of many others lend support to the reality of the event.

The final message of the book is one of love. Scripture contains hundreds of references to love, using four different words for "love" in the Greek: *eros, philia, storge, agape,* and in the Old Testament, the Hebrew word *aheb* for romantic love (*eros*) between humans. The word *philia* is friendship love in the New Testament. It is strong loyalty to friends and family. *Storge* is the loving, natural affection of parents toward their children. In 1 John 4:8, one finds John's ultimate declaration that "God is love" (agape). *Agape* love expresses care and concern for every person on the planet. It is the supreme expression of Christian faith in action.

Agape love is impersonal in the sense that it is directed toward the unfamiliar person: the new arrival, the outsider, the foreigner, the person in front of us at the checkout line. It is a selfless and unconditional love that cares for the welfare of humanity. This love illustrates the essence of God's nature. *Agape* love does not center on one's emotions. Rather, it is an act of the will based upon doing what is right. When teaching of the great commandments, Jesus reminds the listener to first love the Lord your God with all you heart, soul, mind, and strength and then to love your neighbor as yourself.

A sincere expression of *agape* love comes from me to you

in writing this book. I remain fully and passionately committed to the well being of people, not just in attending to temporal needs, but in praying and watching out for their eternal destiny. Locating a model for hell in the solar system is critical to bringing reality to this matter and in avoiding going there. Eternal damnation is a frightening proposition, but God is rich in mercy. He made a way for people to avoid the punishment of hell. By trusting in the atoning work of God's Son, Jesus Christ, we have the right answer, the correct solution to securing our eternal home in heaven.

GLOSSARY OF SCIENTIFIC AND THEOLOGICAL TERMS

Aerospace: The industry concerned with the design and build of flight vehicles, such as aircraft, missiles and spacecraft, which operate in the atmosphere and outer space.

Angular Diameter: The measureable feature of a celestial body in arcseconds or degrees, which gives visual diameter or apparent size as viewed from the earth.

Annihilationism: The belief in unrepentant people not receiving afterlife upon death. The soul or resurrected body of lost individuals will be completely extinguished.

Archimedes' Principle: A law of physics stating that the upward buoyancy force exerted on an immersed body is equivalent to the weight of the displaced fluid.

Artificial Satellite: In spaceflight, man-made objects known as spacecraft, space probes or space vehicles, which are placed in orbit around a celestial body.

Asteroid Belt: The region of space in the solar system between Mars and Jupiter, containing the dwarf planet Ceres and millions of irregular shaped smaller bodies.

Astronomy: The science concerned with the study of celestial objects, including their size, position, motion, geology, and atmospheric environment.

Basalt: A dark, dense, fine-grained igneous rock formed from lava flow. In volcanism, it is the most common rock of extrusion.

Big Bang: The prevailing cosmological concept theorizing the dynamic birth of the universe from an initial singularity. Evidence comes from an expanding universe and the presence of cosmic microwave background radiation (CMBR).

Black Hole: A huge dark object formed by the gravitational collapse of a massive star. The intense gravitational field from the compacted mass prevents particles and even light from being able to escape.

Buoyancy: The upward pressure exerted by a fluid in which a body is immersed.

Cambrian Explosion: The prolific and unparalleled emergence of major classifications of species in the waters of the earth between 540 and 480 million years ago. Before the period, most organisms were simple and composed of only a few cells.

Carboniferous Period: In geological time, the "coal-bearing" period dating from 360 to 290 million years ago. Amphibians and vast swamp land were dominant on the earth during the era.

Cosmic Microwave Background Radiation (CMBR): Thermal radiation emanating from every direction in the universe. The energy is considered as remnant radiant heat from the Big Bang expansion.

Cosmic Rays: High energy radiation in the form of protons or alpha particles with great penetrating power. Primarily originates outside of the solar system.

Cosmochemical Periodic Table of the Elements: A periodic table listing all known chemical elements in the solar system. It supplements the standard periodic table with additional information for each element.

Cosmological Constant: A term introduced by Einstein following his theory of general relativity. The constant is an opposing force to gravity, thought to increase the expansion rate of the universe. It represents a form of dark energy.

Cosmos: The universe as an orderly, complete and harmonious system.

Creationism, divine: The biblical belief in the creation of the cosmos by divine agency. The universe, and all things contained in the natural world, including the various forms of life, was created by God out of nothing (ex nihilo).

Creationism, progressive: The formation of life on Earth by God in separate stages over hundreds of millions of years. The stage represents a day-age from the Genesis creation story, carried out by divine agency. (e.g. Cambrian Explosion).

Crust: The rigid, outermost layer of the earth, which is composed of sedimentary and igneous rock. The expanse covers the continents and the ocean floor.

Dark Energy: A form of energy that is thought to work against the force of gravity. A dominant component of outer space, it may give rise to the increasing expansion rate of the universe.

Dark Matter: A type of matter that cannot be directly observed using conventional imaging or sensing technology. The existence of dark matter is inferred from the various gravitational effects it has on visible matter.

Density: The mass per unit volume of a material substance.

Dispensationalism: A theological approach to the Bible which divides sacred history into a number of specific eras or dispensations. In each dispensation, God deals with humanity in a distinct way.

Eisegesis: The act of reading meaning "into" a biblical text, as opposed to objectively extracting information "out of" a biblical text. (cf. Exegesis)

Electromagnetic Spectrum: The continuum of electromagnetic radiation containing all frequencies of radiation in the universe. The eight classes of radiation include gamma, x-ray, ultraviolet, visible, infrared, terahertz, microwave and radio waves.

Elementary Particle: A component of matter or energy in its simplest form, which cannot be subdivided. Examples include quarks, leptons and bosons.

End of the Age: The understanding of the return of Jesus Christ and God's kingdom to Earth, resulting in a recognizable but sinless environment. There will be a refreshing of the planet, which will contain a familiar sky, solar system, galaxy and universe.

End of the World: The understanding of the return of Jesus Christ and God's kingdom to Earth requiring an eradication of the planet, celestial bodies, and the universe at large, resulting in an unimaginable paradise.

Eschatology: Study concerned with the last events of history. Individual eschatology addresses the final destiny of humanity, including death, judgment, heaven and hell.

Eternal Punishment: The conscious, unending separation from God and from all that is good, given as final judgment to unrepentant people. Physical locations identified in the Bible include Hades, hell, and the lake of fire.

Exegesis: The act of critical interpretation of the biblical text, in order to draw out or explain the meaning of a verse or passage. (cf. Eisegesis)

Event Horizon: The defined boundary of a black hole, where the gravitational pull becomes overpowering and irreversible. Not even photons of light can escape.

Evolution, macro: A major evolutionary transition from one type of organism to another, occurring in large taxonomic groups such as species. The premise provides support to natural evolution.

Evolution, micro: A genetically sound process of secondary or minor evolutionary change within the species, allowing for environmental adaptation and survival.

Evolution, natural: The biological theory formulated by Charles Darwin, accepting that all species develop from a common ancestor, undergo change to advanced anatomies, and persevere through natural selection. Colloquial term is evolution.

Evolution, solar: The formation of the sun and solar system estimated to have begun 4.5 billion years ago from the gravitational collapse of a molecular cloud. The life cycle of the sun will continue in the main sequence phase for 1.5 billion years.

Evolution, theistic: An attempt to harmonize natural evolution with religious teaching by viewing God Himself as directly involved in the biological evolutionary process.

Exegesis: The process of comprehension and explanation of a biblical text, particularly using the historical-critical method, literary interpretation, and reader self-awareness.

Exoplanet: An exoplanet or extrasolar planet is a planetary body orbiting a star outside the solar system.

General Relativity: Einstein's theory of gravitational effects on space, time, matter and energy. General relativity expands upon the theory of special relativity to provide a unified description of gravity as the geometric bending of space-time.

Geocentrism: The astronomical model based on the Ptolemaeus system, where Earth is at the orbital center of all celestial bodies.

Geology: The scientific study of the origin, history, structure and composition of the earth. The field gives evidence for plate tectonics, geological time, climate change, and dating methods (geochronology).

Habitable Zone: The orbital region around a star where a terrestrial or Earth-like planet can retain liquid water on the surface and possibly support life.

Hades: In the New Testament, a place of captivity for the unrighteous, located in the heart of the earth. Lost souls, who are separated from God and from all that is good, await final judgment in Hades. (cf. Sheol)

Hadley Cell: A wind circulation system in the hemispheres where warm air rises near the equator. At high altitude, the air travels toward the poles and cools. It circulates downward and then moves toward the equator to eventually warm up again.

Heaven: The home of God, the holy angels, and those that have attained salvation. It is a place of unsurpassed beauty, supreme happiness, and ultimate fulfillment.

Heaven, celestial: The current location of heaven, where the righteous go after death. The Bible uses the "third heaven" (2 Cor 2:12) or "paradise" (Luke 23:43).

Heaven, on earth: The final locating of heaven to the third planet from the sun. At the end of the age, the return of Jesus will bring a renewing and refreshing to the earth.

Heliocentrism: The cosmological model developed by Copernicus, where Earth and the planets revolve around a stationary sun at the center of the solar system.

Heliosphere: The spherical region of outer space surrounding the sun, which is affected by the solar wind.

Hell: A place of eternal, conscious separation from God and from all that is good. The Greek term for hell is *Gehenna*. It was given as a warning to unrepentant people by Jesus in the gospels. (cf. Lake of Fire)

Hermeneutics: The study of the principles of interpretation, including the written and verbal forms. Applied to the biblical text, hermeneutics would be one method used for understanding truth, value, and meaning.

Immortal Spiritual Body: The eternal state of all humanity, after the final resurrection, promised by Christ. It is an imperishable spiritual body according to 1 Cor. 15:42–4.

Inner Core: The innermost part or center of the earth, consisting of a dense sphere of nickel-iron alloy. The physical properties of the core remain under study.

Intermediate State: The state of existence after one's physical death, which is in the form of a soul. The soul departs the body following physical death and continues in the intermediate state until final resurrection to an immortal spiritual body.

Kuiper Belt: The region of space beyond the orbit of Neptune, which contain the dwarf planets Pluto, Eris, Makemake and Haumea, as well as millions of smaller bodies of icy rock.

Lake of Fire: A place of eternal, conscious separation from God and from all that is good. The sequestering to the lake of fire comes to the unrighteous as a final act of judgment in Rev. 20:11–15. (cf. Hell)

Lava Tube: A natural conduit formed by flowing lava channels. When the outer magna cools and hardens, the inner lava continues to flow, leaving cave-like arteries.

Light Cone: A light cone is the path that a light source takes traveling through space-time. It emanates from a single event and travels in all directions.

Load Cell: A highly sensitive electrical device used for measuring weight. The transducer converts force into an electrical signal using strain gauges.

Magnetosphere: The magnetic field which emanates from the inner earth and extends into outer space. The energy field protects the earth's atmosphere by deflecting the flow of charged particles from the sun (solar wind).

Mantle: The thick stratum of gummy rock below the earth's crust and above the liquid outer core. The mantle divides into two sections, the upper and lower layer.

Mediocrity Principle: A philosophical belief suggesting the complex biological evolution of the earth is not special or exceptional in the overall context of the universe.

Meteor: An object originating from a comet, asteroid, or meteoroid that passes through the earth's atmosphere. Commonly is known as a "shooting star" or "falling star."

Meteorite: A stone, iron or stone-iron object that originates in outer space and reaches the surface of the earth.

Micrometeoroid: An extremely small meteoroid or dust particle traveling at high velocity through space.

Multivalent: In chemistry, the bonding characteristic that is exhibited by the atom of an element. In combination, the element form new chemical compounds.

Nadir: The point directly underfoot a person on the earth. The point 180° opposite is the zenith, which is directly overhead the observer on the earth.

Natural Satellite: A celestial body formed through the natural process of accretion that orbits another body of greater mass, such as a star or planet.

Natural Theology: The belief recognizing that knowledge of God is attainable through nature and the natural order, using human reason. It has been emphasized by the Roman Catholic tradition, owing to the teachings of Thomas Aquinas.

Nebula: A vast cloud of interstellar dust and gas (mainly hydrogen and helium) that is visible through the telescope as a diffuse patch of light.

Old Earth Creationism: A belief in the Genesis creation story taking billions of years. The idea harmonizes with modern scientific thought, especially in regard to physical cosmology, astronomy, chemistry, geology, and the age of the earth.

Orbital Period: For the planets, it is the time required to complete one revolution around the sun. For the earth, the period is approximately 365 ¼ days.

Outer Core: A liquid layer of metal in the heart of the earth that is composed of hot iron and nickel. The molten metal lies below the mantle and above the solid inner core.

Paleontology: The scientific study of life forms in previous geological periods, as represented by plant and animal fossils.

Payload Fairing: The nose cone of a rocket used to protect a spacecraft from the atmospheric launch effects of dynamic pressure and aerodynamic heating.

Phase Diagram: A graph showing the limiting conditions for solid, liquid, and gaseous phases of a particular substance, subject to changes in pressure and temperature.

Photon: The elementary particle or quantum form of electromagnetic radiation. Photons have no rest mass and exhibit wave-particle duality.

Physical Cosmology: The study of the structure and dynamics of the universe that address questions about its origin, formation, evolution, and ultimate fate.

Premillennialism, dispensational: A period in Dispensationalism where Jesus Christ will return to Earth to reign for a period of one thousand years (millennium).

Premillennialism, historic: In eschatology, the belief of Jesus Christ returning to Earth to reign for a period of one thousand years (millennium).

Ptolemaic System: A geocentric physical cosmology of the universe formulated about AD 150 by the Alexandrian astronomer and mathematician Claudius Ptolemaeus.

P-wave: The seismic (primary- or pressure-) wave produced by earthquakes and recorded by seismographs. The longitudinal wave propagation can travel through both the solid and liquid core of the earth.

Quantum Mechanics: The theoretical field of atomic and subatomic particles. Quantum theory interprets the behavior of matter and light, such as wave-particle duality.

Radio Telescope: A parabolic dish antenna used to gather and analyze radio sources from space, including tracking and collecting information from satellites.

Red Shift: An increase in the wavelength of light emitted by an astronomical object, due to movement away from the observer. The color red derives from the elongation of the wave, which moves the observation to the red end of the visible spectrum.

Revelation, divine: The self-disclosure and communication of God to convey knowledge of God to humans. The biblical scriptures provide the practical avenue to make known the divine, which is not accessible to human reason alone.

Revelation, general: The self-disclosure and communication of God in biblical scriptures, as well as through means such as the creation, records of history, philosophy, observation, experience, reason, and innate conscience.

Seismology: The branch of geology concerned with the study of earthquakes and the propagation of seismic waves through the earth.

Sheol: In the Old Testament, a resting place located in the heart of the earth where both the righteous and the unrighteous depart to following death. (cf. Hades)

Sidereal Day: One complete rotation of a planetary body about its axis relative to distant stars, which are used as the reference frame.

Singularity Theorems: In general relativity, the theorems provide a solution to Einstein's field equations, which attempt to postulate singularities and convergence events near the beginning of the universe.

Solar Day: One complete rotation of a planetary body about its axis, wherein the sun returns to the same relative position in the sky.

Solar Wind: The continuous stream of high energy plasma flowing from the sun. The plasma consists of charged particles, mainly electrons and protons.

Soul: The eternal aspects of a person, giving bodily life and vitality. After physical death, the soul departs from the corpse. The soul contains the human personality. The text uses the word "soul" to incorporate both "soul and spirit."

Soul Substance: The material consistency of a soul, likely to be made up of fundamental particles. Soul substance has weight, is subject to the laws of gravity, and contains the genetic makeup or DNA of the individual.

Space-time: The merging of time and three-dimensional space into a four-dimensional continuum. The concept was first proposed in the 1905 theory of special relativity.

Special Relativity: Einstein's theory affirming that physical laws are equally valid for all frames of reference, regardless of relative motion. Makes known the speed of light in a vacuum is a universal constant and discloses the mass-energy equation $E = mc^2$.

Spirit: The conscience of a person, which makes decisions about thoughts and behaviors, performs ethical judgments, and discerns right from wrong.

Steady State Theory: The alternate cosmological theory to the Big Bang, stating the universe is always expanding at a uniform rate with no beginning or end in time.

Stratosphere: The layer of atmosphere directly above the troposphere, extending from 7 to 30 miles above the earth. The ozone layer is found in the stratosphere.

Synthetic Aperture Radar: Synthetic aperture radar (SAR) is a remote sensing and mapping technology, using high energy radio waves that are emitted from an antenna to a target region. SAR systems are normally mounted on an airborne platform, such as an aircraft or spacecraft.

Supercritical Fluid: A substance whose temperature and pressure sits above the critical point of a phase equilibrium diagram. In this condition, the gas and liquid states combine into a single state, with features of each medium being manifest.

S-wave: The seismic (secondary- or shear-) wave produced by earthquakes and recorded by seismographs. The traverse wave propagation can travel through elastic medium, such as the solid core of the earth.

Tribulation Period (Great Tribulation): A term used in eschatology to indicate a seven-year period of suffering prior to the second coming of Jesus Christ (Matt. 24:21, 29-30).

Troposphere: The portion of the atmosphere from ground level to 7 miles above the earth. The planetary boundary layer is the lowest section. The upper section extends to include clouds, water vapor, weather patterns, and the flow of the jet stream.

Universalism: The belief that all humanity will ultimately receive restoration to a right relationship with God. Unrepentant individuals experience a correction and obtain entry in the kingdom of heaven.

Universe: The totality of all space, time, matter, and energy, including planets, moons, minor planets, stars, galaxies, and the contents of intergalactic space. The age of the universe since the time of the Big Bang event is approximately 13.8 billion years.

Virga: A solid or liquid falling from clouds that sublimes or evaporates before reaching the ground.

Volcanism: The process of transferring magma and volatile materials from the interior of a planet by way of volcanic eruption. The phenomenon results in the creation of igneous rock and other lava formations.

Vortex: Rapidly rotating air or liquid moving around a central axis. A vacuum can form in the middle due to the motion, causing the surrounding mass to draw inward.

Word of Knowledge: A spiritual gift wherein divine knowledge is given by the Holy Spirit (1 Cor. 12:7–8). The information is provided for teaching purposes and requires the ability to understand and speak scriptural truth.

Wormhole: A hypothetical passage in space-time, which can connect great distances together in the universe. A traversable wormhole is thought to allow time travel.

X-ray: High energy electromagnetic radiation capable of penetrating solids. It finds extensive use in science and medicine as a diagnostic tool.

Young Earth Creationism: The traditional belief in the creation story of Genesis, accepting a literal six day, (24-hour/day) creation time line. It leaves the Earth to be less than 10,000 years old. The view directly contradicts scientific consensus.

Zenith: The point on the celestial sphere, which is directly overhead an observer on the earth. The point 180° opposite, or directly underfoot, is the nadir.

BIBLIOGRAPHY

Angelo, Joseph A. *Encyclopedia of Space and Astronomy.* New York: Facts on File, Inc., 2006.

Astr 1210 (O'Connell) Study Guide. "Impacts and Bio-Extinctions." http://www. astro.virginia.edu/class/oconnell/ astr121/im/asteroid-impact-frequency-NASA.gif.

Barsukov, V. L. ed. *Venus Geology, Geochemistry and Geophysics: Research Results from the USSR.* Tucson, AZ: University of Arizona Press, 1992.

Bell, Rob. *Love Wins: A Book about Heaven, Hell, and the Fate of Every Person Who Ever Lived.* New York: HarperCollins, 2011.

Bostrom, Nick, and Milan M. Cirkovic, eds. *Global Catastrophic Risks.* New York: Oxford University Press, 2008.

Brainard, Curtis. "The Archeology of the Stars." *New York Times: Science Times*, February 11, 2014: 1–2.

Burgess, Eric. *Venus: An Errant Twin.* New York: Columbia University Press, 1985.

California Institute of Technology (Caltech). "Planets Abound." http://www.caltech. edu/content/planets-abound.

Cao, A., and B. Romanowicz. "Constraints on Shear Wave Attenuation in the Earth's Inner Core from an Observation of PKJKP." *Geophysical Reserch Letters* 36, no. 9 (May 2009): 5.

CIA World Factbook. "Library Publications: People and Society." https://www.cia. gov/library/publications/the-world-factbook/ geos/xx.html.

Chadwick, Henry, trans. *Saint Augustine Confessions.* New York: Oxford University Press, 1998.

Coogan, Michael D., ed. *The New Oxford Annotated Bible: New Revised Standard Version.* New York: Oxford University Press, 2001.

Crockett, William, ed. *Four Views on Hell.* Grand Rapids, MI: Zondervan, 1992.

Draper, Warren F., trans. *The Book of Enoch.* Andover, MA: U.S. Act of Congress, 1882.

Elwell, Walter A., ed. *Baker Encyclopedia of the Bible.* Grand Rapids, MI: Baker Book House, 1988.

Encyclopedia Britannica. "*Primary Wave.*" http://www.britannica. com/EBchecked/ topic/476245/primary-wave.

Gonzalez, Guillermo, and Jay W. Richards. *The Privileged Planet: How Our Place in the Cosmos Is Designed for Discovery.* Washington, DC: Regnery, 2004.

GotQuestions.org. "What are Some Modern Forms of Idolatry?" http://www.got questions.org/idolatry-modern.html.

Greeley, Ronald. *Lava Tubes in the Solar System.* 6th International Symposium on Vulcanospeleology. Tempe, AZ: Arizona State University Planetary Geology Group, 1992.

Grinspoon, David H. *Venus Revealed: A New Look Below the Clouds of Our Mysterious Twin Planet.* Reading, MA: Addison-Wesley, 1997.

Hawking, Stephen W., and George F. R. Ellis. "The Cosmic Black-Body Radiation and the Existence of Singularities in Our Universe." *Astrophysical Journal* 152, (1968): 25–36.

Hawking, Stephen, and Roger Penrose. "The Singularities of Gravitational Collapse and Cosmology." *Proceedings of the Royal Society of London*, Series A, 314 (1970): 529-48.

Hawking, Stephen W. *A Brief History of Time.* New York: Bantam Books, 1998.

Hodge, Charles. *Systematic Theology, Vol. III.* http://www.ccel. org /ccel/hodge/theology3.

International Astronomical Union. "Resolution B5: Definition of a Planet in the Solar System." XXVIth IAU General Assembly (26th). Prague, Czech Republic: IAU, August 24, 2006. 1.

———. IAU 2006 General Assembly: Result of the IAU Resolution Votes. http://www.iau.org/public_press/news/detail/iau0603/.

Ishida, Masayoshi. "Rebuttal to Claimed Refutations of Duncan MacDougall's Experiment on Human Weight Change at the Moment of Death." *Journal of Scientific Exploration* 24, no. 1 (Spring 2010): 5–39.

John F. Kennedy Presidential Library and Museum. "Excerpt from an Address Before a Joint Session of Congress, 25 May 1961." http://www.jfklibrary.org/ Asset-Viewer/xzw1gaeeTES6khED14P1lw.aspx.

Keathley, J. Hampton. "The Pauline Epistles." http://bible.org/seriespage/pauline-epistles.

LaHaye, Tim, and Ed Hinson, eds. *The Popular Encyclopedia of Bible Prophecy.* Eugene, OR: Harvest House, 2004.

Lewis, C. S. *The Great Divorce.* New York: MacMillan, 1946.

MacDougall, Duncan. "Hypothesis Concerning Soul Substance Together with Experimental Evidence of the Existence of Such Substance." *American Society for Physical Research* 1, no. 5 (May 1907): 237–44.

Moore, Patrick. *Venus.* London: Octopus Publishing, 2002.

NASA. "Giant Black Hole Rips Apart Unlucky Star in Cosmic Reality Show." http://www.nasa.gov/home/hqnews/2004/feb/HQ_04061_black_hole.html.

———. "How Do We Know When Voyager Reaches Interstellar Space?" http://www.jpl.nasa.gov/news/news.php?release=2013-278.

National Academy of Sciences of the United States of America Proceedings. "Prevalence of Earth-size Planets Orbiting Sun-like Stars." http://www.pnas.org/ content/110/48/19273.

New York Times. "Spacecraft Spots Active Volcanoes on Venus." http://www. nytimes.com/2010/04/10/science/space/10venus.html.

Peterson, Robert A. *Hell on Trial: The Case for Eternal Punishment.* Phillipsburg, NJ: Presbyterian and Reformed Publishing, 1995.

Reasons to Believe. "Does Macroevolution Fit the Fossil Record?" http://www.reasons.org/explore/topic/evolution.

———. "The Waters of the Flood." http://www.reasons.org/articles/the-waters-of-the-flood.

Russell, C. T. et.al. "Lightning on Venus Inferred from Whistler-mode Waves in the Ionosphere." *Nature* 450, no. 7170 (2007): 661–62.

Russell, Robert John. *Cosmology: From Alpha to Omega.* Minneapolis, MN: Fortress Press, 2008.

———. *Time in Eternity: Pannenberg, Physics and Eschatology in Creative Mutual Interaction.* Notre Dame, IN: University of Notre Dame Press, 2012.

Russell, Robert John, William R. Stoeger, SJ, and George V. Coyre SJ. *Physics, Philosophy and Theology: A Common Quest for Understanding.* Vatican City State: Vatican Observatory Publications, 1988.

Ryrie, Charles C. *A Survey of Bible Doctrine.* Chicago: Moody Publishers, 1972.

Saint Thomas Aquinas. *Summa Theologica.* New York: Benziger Brothers, 1947.

Shearer, Peter M., Catherine A Rycher, and Qinya Liu. "On the Visibility of the Inner-core Shear Wave Phase PKJKP at Long Periods." *Geophysics Journal International* 185, no. 3 (2011): 1379–83.

Song, Xiaodong. "Anisotropy of the Earth's Inner Core." Washington, DC.: American Geophysical Union, August 1997. *Reviews of Geophysics* 35, no. 3 297-313.

Sproul, R.C. *The Consequences of Ideas: An Overview of Philosophy.* Orlando, FL: Ligonier Ministries, 1998.

Svedhem, Hakan; Dmitry V. Titov; Fredric W. Taylor; and Olivier Witasse. "Venus as a More Earth-like Planet." *Nature* 450, No. 7170 (2007): 629–32.

University of Hamburg English Department. "A Virtual Introduction to Science Fiction: Online Toolkit for Teaching SF." http://virtual-sf.com/.

Walvoord, John F., and Roy B. Zuck. *The Bible Knowledge Commentary.* Colorado Springs, CO: David C. Cook Publisher, 2002.

Ward, Peter D., and Donald Brownlee. *Rare Earth: Why Complex Life Is Uncommon in the Universe.* New York: Copernicus Books, 2004.

Wiese, Bill. *23 Minutes in Hell.* Lake Mary, FL: Charisma House, 2006.

Wikipedia. "Duncan MacDougall." http://en.wikipedia.org/wiki/Duncan_MacDougall _ (doctor)

INDEX OF SCRIPTURE

General Index

solar wind, 142, 143

solitary confinement, 126, 174, 178

soul. *See also* departed souls; intermediate state; lost souls

  body, soul, and spirit, 103*f*

  confinement of in Hades, 119–27

  as having physical mass, 92

  and immortal spiritual body, 102–7

  resurrection of, 171

  soul sleep, 34, 35n21

  soul substance. *See* soul substance

  as transitional state, 47

soul sleep, 34, 35n21

soul substance, 107–19, 124, 125, 171

South Pole, 149n88

Soviet spacecraft, 8, 11n6

space exploration, 17, 18, 20, 21–23, 141

Space Patrol, 138

Space Shuttle (STS-1), 22, 25, 157

spacecraft design and operation, 23–26

space-time, 14, 62, 71n38, 74–77, 180

The Space Trilogy (Lewis), 138

special relativity, theory of, 74–75, 76

speed of light in a vacuum, 62, 75, 75n44, 143, 179

spirit, 103, 103*f*, 104

spiritual gifts, 5n4

spiritual world, 105*f*

spirituality, role of, 57

spring tension scales, 109n59

Sputnik 1, 21

Sputnik 2, 21

SS *Atlantis*, 157

stars, 64, 81. *See also* evening star; morning star

static universe, 70

steady state theory, 70, 71

stellar archeology, 64

stellar evolutionary process, 83

storge (love), 184

STS-1 (Space Shuttle), 22, 25, 157

sulfur, 9, 10, 11, 132, 153, 155, 156, 161, 167

sulfur cycle, 11, 152–53

sun

  future of, 91, 92

  as G-type main sequence star, 83

sunspots, 142

supernatural, superimposing of, 63, 87

synthetic aperture radar (SAR), 129, 157, 157n93

T

ta ethne (nations), 45

tartaroo (cast into hell/cast into Tartarus), 99

Tartarus, 98*f*, 99, 125

telescopes

  Hubble Space Telescope, 2, 18

  radio telescopes, 60, 138, 143

temporal physical body, 105*f*, 107

temporary confinement, 99, 126

terra (land/earth), 20

terrestrial planets, 20

Than'-at-os (Death), 12

theistic evolution, 67, 68

theology

  biblical theology, 61*f*, 73

  natural theology, 3–4

  theological development, 48, 48n28

theoretical astronomy, 60

theory of general relativity, 60, 75

theory of special relativity, 74–75, 76

third heaven, 105

time (t), 72–74

Toledo Computer Scale Company, 109

Tophet, in Jeremiah, 13

transit event, 10, 134, 135, 136

tribulation period, 84, 99, 171

trumpet blowing, 84n53, 99, 101, 153

Tunguska event, 82n52

23 Minutes in Hell (Weiss), 120-121, 124

U

universal physical constant (c), 62

universal resurrection, 49, 105

universal salvation, 52

universal space, immortal spiritual body as residing within, 28n14

universalism, 49, 51–52, 53, 54, 179

universe, 2, 3, 4, 15, 16, 22, 52, 55–65, 68–92, 94, 107, 139, 179

unquenchable fire, 5n3, 10, 35, 133, 144, 167

unrighteous, 2, 12, 16, 31, 32, 33, 34, 36, 39, 40, 48, 50, 51, 61, 104, 105, 106, 125, 129, 132, 133, 139, 155, 161, 167, 170

Uranus, 18, 19

V

Vanguard 1, 21

Vega missions, 156

Venera 4, 144

Venera 7, 145, 146

Venera 8, 145, 146

Venera 9, 146, 147, 147f, 170

Venera 10, 146

Venera 11, 148, 150

Venera 12, 148, 150

Venera 13, 150, 151, 151f

Venera 14, 150, 152

Venera missions/program, 8, 154, 155, 156

Venus

abodes on, 160

atmosphere of, 11, 156

as place of perdition, 17, 159

compared to Hades, 177t

demonic beings sent to, 97

as evening star, 129, 132, 135

as final destination of Satan, 16

as final destiny of unsaved people, 53

four thermal zones of, 153n89, 154, 156, 157, 159

future of, 83

gender assigned to, 138

gravitational force, 107

as hell and lake of fire, 15, 51, 179

as improved venue over Hades, 127, 174

as morning star, 129, 131, 132

naming of, 129–30

orbital and physical characteristics of, 166–68

orbital path, 130, 131f, 132

as place of loss and sadness, 91

polar cloud top of, 149f

radiation from, 138–39

as seen through telescope, 133–141

as sister/twin to Earth, 129

solar day on, 140–41

surface of, 8, 10, 127, 147f, 147–48, 151f, 151–152

surface temperature of, 143

as target of spaceflights, 22
as terrestrial planet, 20
upper atmosphere of, 153
zonal and meridional circulation,
  164f
Venus Express, 150, 154, 163,
  164, 166
Venus Geology, Geochemistry and
  Geophysics: Research Results
  from the USSR, 156
Venus Spectral Rocket (VeSpR),
  166
The Venus International Reference
  Atmosphere (Advances in Space
  Research), 152
vignette of afterlife on Venus,
  170–75
visions, 6
volcanism, 10, 121, 148, 159, 162
vortex, 149f, 149–50, 165–66

Vostok 1, 21, 22
Voyager 1, 142n83

W
Weiss, Bill, 120, 124
Wheatstone bridge, 113n64
whistler wave, 154
Wikipedia, 112
Wilson, Robert, 78
Word of Knowledge, 5–6
wormhole, 179, 180

X
x-ray fluorescent spectrometer,
  11n6, 150

Y
yôm (day), 62, 63
young earth creationism, 62, 87

Printed in the United States
by Baker & Taylor Publisher Services